HOW TO PASS *ANY* EXAM

Brian Duncalf was born and bred in the shadow of one of Manchester's dark satanic mills. When he was sixteen financial trouble 'at t' mill' made his father redundant, so he left school to become the only wage-earner in a family of four.

In industry, he discovered he couldn't get far without a degree, so he enrolled on an evening course which – after nine years and sometimes four evening classes a week – led to the coveted qualification. He later obtained a Ph.D. through part-time study while working in a full-time job.

Now a retired teacher, he lives near Hereford and devotes his time to writing, photography and compiling crossword puzzles.

D1483814

HOW TO PASS *ANY* EXAM

Brian Duncalf

KYLE CATHIE LIMITED

▼

Dedication

To my wife Sue, without whose encouragement and help this book would never have been started, let alone finished.

First published in Great Britain in 1994 by
Kyle Cathie Limited
20 Vauxhall Bridge Road, London SW1V 2SA

Reprinted 1994
New edition 1996
Reprinted 1997

ISBN 1 85626 237 5

A CIP catalogue record for this book is available from the British Library.

Typeset by York House Typographic Ltd.
Printed and bound by Cox & Wyman Ltd., Reading

Contents

▼

Acknowledgements

I would like to acknowledge the contribution made by my past students over the years. Their exam scripts and comments during 'exam tutorials' not only demonstrated the need for this book, but also provided much of its content. Thanks also to Gwendoline Hewett of the Associated Examining Board and to John Pady of the Driving Standards Agency.

A very special 'thank you' is offered to Lady Thatcher, Sir Anthony Hopkins and to Richard Branson for their generous contribution of personal details of some of their early academic efforts. Caroline Taggart also deserves my sincere thanks for her efficient and constructive editing of my manuscript. Last, and certainly not least, to Claire Rayner for sharing my faith in the need for this book.

▼

Introduction

It is not what you do, it's the way that you do it.

In many cases, the outcome of an examination is decided long before the candidate enters the examination room. No, the examiner has not previously chosen who will pass and who will fail. It is the *candidate* who has 'decided'. It is all to do with preparation.

In Britain in 1992 over five million examination scripts were written for GCSE examinations alone. Without sound advice, each of the candidates will have made at least one blunder in preparing for and sitting each examination. The previous year the same blunders were made. In fact, every year the same blunders are made. Over ten million *avoidable* blunders every year! And that's just in GCSE exams. The situation becomes even more serious if we look at a broader picture. For over forty years I have studied students' examination techniques from the standpoint of both examinee and examiner, and I have found that, in many cases, students in colleges are no better informed. So, what is to be done? We can't avoid examinations. They are a fact of life – alas, say many people. In any modern, progressive community there is hardly a family that doesn't have at least one member engaged in examinations of some sort at one time or another. Over the last few decades, examinations have become as much a part of our lives as supermarkets and television.

Now here's a paradox. Television, magazines, books and evening classes offer courses of instruction for people who want to keep fit, lose weight or improve their posture. There are even courses on childbirth. And yet, for thousands of years, all these things have been regarded as a natural part of life. So today we seem to need instruction on how to cope with natural aspects of life! But exams. What could be more unnatural? Yet where is the instruction for those who suffer from these totally unnatural contrivances of Man? How many TV programmes deal with exams? How many magazines? How many books? While it is true that there are books and crash courses for specific subjects, there seems to be very little guidance on the general techniques which are common to all examinations, irrespective of the subject.

This book is intended to make up for that deficiency. But how? You will find neither revision notes nor sample exam papers here. Partly this is for reasons of practicality, because no one book could hope to cover every subject adequately. But, more to the point, they are not needed because the answer to the problem of exams – any exams – is much simpler than that, as we shall see.

The quotation at the beginning of this Introduction may seem a bit casual, but it does represent an important point. Let us think about it.

I am sure that most of us know at least one person who likes to relate funny stories, but does it very badly. He tells a story in his usual style and it takes off like a lead balloon. Nobody laughs. We probably also know another person with a better technique. He tells the same story and everyone folds up in laughter. It's not what they do, it's the way that they do it.

Driving a car is simple. Your left foot is used on the clutch pedal. Your right foot operates the accelerator, and sometimes the brake. Your hands control the steering wheel and one is occasionally used to change gear. Everybody drives a car like this. There is no other way. And yet some people are terrible drivers and others are superb. It's not what they do, it's the way that they do it.

Tackling examinations is no different. Believe me, there are bad ways and there are good ways. With the bad ways you can spend lots and lots of time and hard work in preparation, and you can still fail.

Let me tell you about the good ways. Adopt them and you are virtually guaranteed to pass, for that is what this book is all about!

Chapter 1

▼

Why Have Examinations?

Any fool can ask questions. What is clever is giving the right answers.
Brian Duncalf

Very few people actually *enjoy* examinations. Most of us dislike the things intensely. All the revision, hard work and anxiety don't seem to be of any real value. Some people feel sick at the thought of preparing for and sitting exams, and some actually are!

Another thing. Have you noticed that when the time comes to revise for exams, the weather improves and we often have great sunny spells and heat waves?

It's all the examiners' fault, of course.

Or is it?

At some time or another, we have all thought of examiners as evil, sadistic monsters who simply love to find every tiny error in exam scripts and put big black crosses against them, muttering something like, 'Good. Here's another one I can fail.'

Naturally, they started out by thinking of the sort of questions that would trip up candidates, reveal their weaknesses and make them squirm. They set trick questions and used any devious method they could think of to fail as many candidates as possible.

Yes. Most of us have thought of examiners in these terms. But now, let us think again and this time let us be fair. Let us ask the question 'What are exams actually *for*?'

To answer this one we must first ask why go to school,

or college or, for that matter, to a polytechnic or university? Do we do it for fun? Some do, but the large number do it for other reasons.

Children do it because they are *made* to, but later in life they realise that there is more to education than simply getting them from under Mum's feet. Sooner or later most of us have to earn our keep.

There are two major reasons why the more mature people choose to educate themselves beyond the legal requirements. One is because they actually *enjoy* their chosen subject and want to learn as much as possible about it (and even practise it as much as possible). Such people are indeed fortunate, but even they are sometimes bedevilled by the need to study ancillary subjects which are imposed upon them by their educators. But more of this later.

Let us look at the other main reason why people study. To qualify them for a career.

Some decades ago, people who wanted a job would have to learn the skills required under a suitable master. They would serve an apprenticeship, study and practise for years, until, eventually, they themselves became master craftsmen. But all of this involved *practical* skills, which could, more often than not, be judged by the results of their labours. You could see if a wheelwright had produced a decent wheel or if a clock mender had made your clock work.

This applies only to a small extent these days. For example, after a car is serviced, can you tell whether the mechanic was a good one or not? Was the electrician who wired your house good at his job, or is the insurance salesman *really* as knowledgeable about insurance as he would have you believe?

These people can't always be judged by the appearance of their work. Sometimes their work can't be seen, so how can their qualities as professionals be assessed?

The answer to this should be obvious. These people can be judged by their qualifications. And to obtain qualifications they had to pass exams. Those examinations have become essential to our modern way of life. (Do I hear some of you say, 'More's the pity'?)

Let's face it, few of us would go to a doctor who was not qualified. It is expected of a doctor that he or she will have spent some years studying Medicine and will have passed examinations to prove it. So when you practise *your* profession (either now or in the future), hasn't *your* client (or customer, or whatever) the right to expect that you are adequately qualified also? If you work for (or are to work for) a larger organisation with many employees, hasn't your employer the right to expect that you are (or will be) competent in your chosen profession?

You can see where all this is leading, can't you? Yes. Get qualified. And how? By passing those examinations!

Before we go any further, let us try a bit of role reversal. Suppose that *you* are an employer and you are looking for an employee to fill some specific position in the firm and to carry out their duties satisfactorily.

What do you look for?

Well, there are certain professions where the qualifications can be demonstrated on a practical level. A photographer, for example, can carry a portfolio to illustrate the sort of work of which he is capable. A designer can do the same. A chauffeur can demonstrate his skills by driving; a model is a living example of her (or his) abilities in that particular field of work and a translator can easily prove his or her skills with the spoken or written word.

However, many abilities cannot be demonstrated in this way. A nurse could not do it, nor a chemist. Accountants, surveyors, computer programmers and a host of others too numerous to mention would all be in grave difficulties trying to prove their worth (in a reasonable period of time, that is).

So how would *you* choose between competing candidates? By appearance? By the way the candidates talk? Both of these are important, of course, but they don't tell you much about the knowledge or skills of the applicant. For these, something more objective and searching is required.

Obviously, another means of finding out about a candidate's abilities is to let someone else do it for you. An examiner for example. At each stage of a person's development in a particular field, an examiner can test their knowledge and/or abilities by means of examinations. Having reached a certain level of competence, the person can then be allowed to move to the next stage of his education and be assessed again, and so on.

Notice that expression 'certain level of competence'. It is an important term. I didn't say, for example, 'perfection'. Many examination candidates seem to think that they are not allowed to make *any* mistakes in examinations and this stance can seriously undermine their confidence. Edward John Phelps summed this up neatly when he said, 'The man who makes no mistakes does not usually make anything.' All that an examiner is looking for is a demonstration that the candidate has learned enough from his education to be regarded as being *of a satisfactory standard* (often, to proceed further).

So you, as the prospective employer, may decide to ask for candidates to have completed the first year at the Ordinary (or Higher) Certificate level in the required subject. A candidate who has passed such an examination is likely to be better equipped to do the job in question than one who hasn't.

This, then, is one of the reasons for examinations. To give an *indication* of the competence of an applicant for a particular job or position. However, this is not the be-all and end-all of the matter, there is much more to examination results than that.

▶ Ancillary Subjects ◀

What about exams in ancillary subjects? Why are *they* so important? Let us try to find out.

Supposing that you go to a restaurant for a meal. The chef may be virtually perfect in the matter of preparing a fillet steak to your requirements, but would you be happy if he had no idea at all about health and hygiene? Would you be happy in the knowledge that he had just sliced your partner's boiled ham on the same machine that had previously been used to cut some uncooked meat (with the likelihood of bacterial contamination from the latter)? It is not sufficient for a chef to know how to prepare food. He (or she) must also know about all other aspects of food preparation and the *ancillary* subjects related thereto. Hence, a knowledge of how bacteria grow and thrive and how they can contaminate food is just as important as an ability to cook.

Similarly, an architect designing a bridge could hardly be said to be competent if his mathematical ability was so limited that he could not calculate the stresses involved in a bridge he had designed. It might look good, but would it be *safe*?

Another reason for having ancillary subjects is to avoid the problem of following too deep a rut in one's speciality. Topics called Liberal Studies, General Studies, Supporting Studies or some other such title may be included to broaden the mind and minimise the possibility of becoming too narrow in outlook. But should you be examined in these subjects? Well, you would hardly do justice to these subjects if you were not examined. And if you didn't take them seriously, you wouldn't reap the intended benefit from them. Would you?

Now, what about the person who says, 'All I want to be is a car mechanic. I don't *need* all those other subjects, I'll be happy for the rest of my life simply looking after car engines'? Is this a valid reason for not studying any other subject?

Absolutely *not*!

Why? Because things change and people change. We all do. It's inevitable. Many *think* that they won't, but they do.

I could quote dozens of examples of students of mine who thought that they knew *exactly* what they wanted in life, and had no intention of changing it. At that moment they were right, of course, but life has a funny habit of changing things for you.

We all need a challenge. The problem is, once we have met and matched up to that challenge, it then ceases to be a challenge any more! We then need a *further* challenge. *We* have changed.

Let's get back to our theoretical car mechanic.

After a few years of looking after car engines, he finds that, perhaps, he wants something a little more taxing. Perhaps a different make of car. Perhaps the larger engines of commercial machines. Or maybe he just needs more money coming in. You can't get more money doing the same old job (not much anyway). You have to change jobs. But the rate of pay for car mechanics at one firm is not all that different from the rate at other firms. No, you have to change *direction*. You may have to become a supervisor in another garage, or you may have to go into sales (of cars). But there is always the possibility that you will have to go into another type of job altogether and for that you will need qualifications.

It has often been said that a person with a university degree only uses about one or two per cent of the knowledge which was acquired in order to get that degree. If the graduate *knew* which part of the subject he or she would need, then the time spent in studying for the degree could be cut down enormously. However, life doesn't work that way. Jobs change, and the knowledge required for those jobs changes accordingly. But the fact that a person has a degree means that he *has* the knowledge to adjust to the new job. That is what the qualification is all about. We study an over-wide spectrum in order to be able to apply our knowledge over a wide field, and when we are studying, we don't know *where* in that field we are going to need the knowledge. The wider the field studied, the wider the scope for application and the bigger the area in which we can be employed.

There is another point to be considered here, too. How often have we heard someone say something like, 'He has a degree in Social Sciences (or whatever), how does that qualify him to be in charge of a travel agency?' The answer lies not so much in the subject studied as in the *method* of study. If the study has been systematic and objective, then the same logical principles used in that study can be applied in *any other* area. The principle is not *what* he studied, but rather that he *studied*!

Quite simply, the process of studying improves the mind and an improved mind is a more versatile mind.

▶ Examination Pressure ◀

A constant complaint about examinations is that they produce stress, and that, under' stress, the candidate cannot perform at his (or her) best. Therefore exams are unfair.

It won't do, you know! This is no justifiable criticism of exams. Here's why.

Life is full of stresses. Life would be very boring *without* some stress, as a happy life is one with *variety*. Life needs ups and downs if it is not to become monotonous.

But what (you may ask) has this got to do with exams?

Well, a potential employer needs to know not only whether his new employee has enough knowledge to do the job, but also whether he can *do* the job under the conditions which are likely to prevail in practice? This stance is not an unreasonable one. It is no good having a very knowledgeable employee who goes to pieces as soon as pressure is applied. Because pressure *will* be applied, whether you like it or not. Life is like that.

So, then, a qualification not only demonstrates that a person has studied satisfactorily, but also that he has coped with the stress that is incurred in taking examinations: a person who can cope with this sort of stress is more likely to be able to deal with other kinds of pressure than one who can't.

In other words, a qualification obtained by taking examinations is also *some* indication of a person's ability to match up to the problems that occur in real-life situations.

Changing Horses – Successfully!

The saying 'Don't change horses in the middle of a stream' is not always the best advice.

I had just finished a tutorial with a group of twenty-year-old students on a day-release course when one of them approached me in a state of some distress. It seemed that I had, quite unwittingly, brought to his attention something which he had not considered before.

I had been stressing that the 'How?' of what you do is not as important as the 'Why?' because, as materials change, the techniques used to handle them must also change. I added that there would be a lot of changes in the next forty to forty-five years of their working lives. This last point was the cause of his concern.

His job was very well paid, but he felt that his role in life was rather pointless. He wanted to help people. In fact, he wanted to be a nurse, but nobody had taken him seriously.

It was not up to me to persuade him to stay on the course or, for that matter, to leave it. All that I could do was to help him to focus his attention on the *quality* of his life, and what he really wanted to do with it.

He left the course at the end of that session.

About two years later he called into the college to see me. He had never been happier, he told me. The money he earned was hardly comparable to what he would have earned in the industry he had left, but he felt that he was helping people. More importantly, his life had meaning, which it had lacked before.

Was he a failure because he didn't complete the course? I hardly think so. To my way of thinking he was more of a success than many (wealthier) people I know.

He hadn't wasted his time on my course, either. The science content that he had successfully completed was accepted on the nursing course, so he didn't have to waste his time repeating that material.

Finally, it would appear that examinations are with us to stay, so whether we like it or not, we have to learn to deal with them. And they should not really become all that traumatic. Using the right techniques to tackle exams will minimise the work involved and maximise the likelihood of success. So don't be frightened of exams, just approach them the right way!

▶ Summary ◀

1. The competence of some people can be judged by the products of their labours. For others, examination successes provide the most commonly accepted alternative.
2. The public expects, and is entitled to expect, that members of certain professions have qualified by examination in the principal subject and in essential ancillary subjects.
3. Most employers consider examination successes a valuable indication of the suitability of job applicants.
4. Proven ability to cope with exam stresses indicates a certain likelihood of being able to cope with life's stresses.

Chapter 2

▼

'Passes' and 'Fails'

You cannot be a failure if you are still trying.
Brian Duncalf

At one time, examination candidates waited for what appeared to be interminable ages for the dreaded exam results. When they came, they were often simple statements of fact: 'Pass' or 'Fail'. Occasionally passes were qualified with a 'with Credit' or 'with Distinction', but the so-called 'failed' candidates didn't know whether they had failed by two marks or thirty-two. They had simply failed.

In many cases, today, the situation is somewhat different. Candidates may still wait weeks or even months for their results, but now they are graded according to their performance. They may be awarded an 'A' or an 'F' (or whatever the system dictates).

Neither system is the best or the worst. They are simply different. And each needs to be put into its proper context.

The all-or-nothing system of 'pass' or 'fail' left much to be desired for anyone who had not passed the exam. A failed candidate had no indication of *how* badly he (or she) had done.

At first glance the other system of grading the exam scores *seems* to be better. But is it? How good, for example, is a grade C pass compared to a grade D? Would publishing the actual marks give a better indication of the candidate's performance?

We have already discovered (from Chapter 1) that the overall purpose of an examination is to test whether the student has benefited sufficiently from the tuition received. The word 'sufficiently' is the crux of the matter, of course. Who, for example, is to say what mark corresponds to a 'pass' or a 'fail'? Sometimes a mark of forty is sufficient for a 'pass'. In other areas fifty is regarded as the minimum. The problem from the standpoint of the candidate is that different examining bodies have different standards, and those standards are not always made public. Even if they were, few candidates would be in a better position, because many are not aiming at a particular mark, but rather at a satisfactory performance in the exam (or exams) as a whole.

At this point, it may be worth considering the plight of the *examiner*. He (or she) is supposed to be in the privileged position of deciding who 'passes' and who 'fails'. Believe me, privilege has nothing to do with it! The examiner has the very unenviable task of trying to be fair to all the examinees. Contrary to popular belief, examiners *do* try to be fair, and they prefer, by and large, to pass candidates rather than fail them, but the performance in the exam *must* be the basis on which they make their judgement.

Both the so-called 'pass mark' and the examiner have a lot to answer for. They are supposed to provide a line of demarcation between candidates who are 'satisfactory' and those who are not. It is not easy, and anyone who thinks that it is should attempt a little test for themselves. Try dividing all the films that you have ever seen into 'good' and 'bad'. That's all – no 'OK', no 'about average', just good and bad. The *very* good ones and the *very* bad ones should be fairly easy to distinguish. But then there is a grey area in between where the division is not so clearcut. If you are honest, you will find that it is not easy to 'play at God' and make important decisions of this kind. You are lucky. Your decision on films doesn't really matter. Nobody will suffer. But the examiner's decision *does* matter. It could make all the difference to somebody's future education or career.

In other words, the difference between a pass and a fail can be minimal, and shouldn't be the cause of undue elation or despair.

▶ What is a pass? ◀

Many candidates, having received the exam result of 'pass', feel that everything is well. The preparation and work involved have finally paid off and resting on laurels or celebrating at the pub is the order of the day. This is OK, but remember that the 'pass' may be *only just* a pass!

The problem sometimes crops up when someone says, 'He's supposed to have a degree in . . . and I know more about it than he does!' This may well be true, because having a degree in a given subject doesn't mean you know everything there is to know about it.

Any qualification means that the possessor has reached a certain standard and *nothing more*. The possessor of a degree is *not* the world's expert in his field. A graduate has demonstrated a certain level of knowledge and understanding, but that is all. Moreover, the wise graduate realises how much he *doesn't* know and acknowledges that even if he studied for the remainder of his life, he would never know all there was to be known – even in his own specialised subject.

▶ What is a fail? ◀

The term 'fail' is a much misunderstood one and needs to be looked at carefully. It is used to indicate a failure *to reach a satisfactory standard*. It does *not* mean that the candidate is an out-and-out failure in life, or anything else for that matter.

It is possible for anyone to fail an examination. There can be dozens of reasons for this, so let's take a look at the more common ones.

▶ Lack of interest ◀

A student who is not interested in a subject is obviously less likely to study that subject satisfactorily than if he were interested in it and is, therefore, less likely to give a creditable performance in the exam. That raises the question, 'Why is the student taking the exam at all?' The answer often lies in the attitudes of other people: teachers, parents and, in the case of more mature students, husbands or wives. Each of these parties may have their own reasons for pushing a person in a certain direction, though these reasons are not always beyond criticism. Arguments such as 'Your father never had the chance to study Latin, but you have' or 'You come from generations of engineers' are often used as psychological blackmail, and can cause unnecessary stress and unhappiness.

On the other hand, literacy and numeracy are essential in the modern world, so a lack of interest in English or Mathematics just has to be overcome. The same applies to certain aspects of the National Curriculum and to ancillary subjects in some courses. You simply have to resign yourself to the fact that, unpalatable as it may be, the work in these subjects must be done.

▶ The subject is 'too difficult' ◀

No subject should be 'too difficult' for an examination candidate, because no student should be allowed to prepare for an examination which is beyond his capabilities. Once again, the responsibility for this often lies with others. An entrance examination or, in some cases, the quality of course work, should indicate a student's potential and the likelihood of success in exams. Steps should be taken at an early stage to ensure that the candidate is not over-taxed. This is especially important when a large number of examinations is to be taken. If you feel that you, or your child, are simply not coping, see the tutor

Failing exams need not be a disaster

Candidates sometimes become obsessed with passing every examination which they sit. It is a noble ambition and one to be encouraged. However, the *thought* of failing a single exam may be more distressing than a failure itself. This needs to be brought into context.

When a series of examinations is being taken for a qualification (a diploma or degree, say), it is often necessary to pass every exam or to gain a certain minimum number of 'credits'. If these are the regulations, then you have no alternative but to comply.

When *single* subjects are being taken (such as with secondary education), the situation is different. Candidates may be required to sit examinations in subjects in which they have little interest. Such lack of interest does not constitute a legitimate excuse for not trying, but if you make a *genuine* effort and still fail, you must not regard yourself as one of life's failures.

At school, a certain youth passed his O level GCE in English Literature but failed in Maths, Geography, History, Sciences, French, Latin and all sport and PE. However, he did not allow this to stand in his way, but went on to pursue matters of greater interest to him. He is now known to millions as a star of stage and screen.

His name is Sir Anthony Hopkins.

and talk your problems through. (We'll look at this in more detail in Chapter 3.)

There is another point which needs emphasis here. A subject which is 'too difficult' at one time may not always be so. It is a matter of selection, interest or background. For example, a person with a limited knowledge of

Mathematics is hardly likely to be able to cope with a mathematically based subject at degree level, but this does not mean that the same person will always be in that position. The degree of 'difficulty' of a subject varies with a person's experience and education.

▶ Unsatisfactory Revision ◀

'Nerves' are often blamed for poor examination performances and this may be true in some cases. However, if this is excluded for the moment (it is dealt with in Chapter 6), unsatisfactory revision is likely to be a more common cause – especially with those candidates who are eager to do well in their chosen subjects.

The term 'unsatisfactory', when applied to revision, covers both quality and quantity, and, on occasion, one can depend upon the other. The following list covers the major causes of unsatisfactory revision.

a. Too many subjects being examined

b. Other demands on time

c. Leaving revision until too late

d. Poor revision technique

Let us consider these point by point.

▶ Too Many Subjects ◀

Some candidates appear to believe that the more exams they take, the better their chances of gathering at least *some* qualifications. The validity of this philosophy depends very much on the individual student.

It is true that some people are able to take a large number of examinations in their stride, apparently without any excessive effort. Others struggle with a few. As individuals vary, there can be no hard and fast rule about this, but what each student needs to do is to make a serious effort to assess his true potential. With subjects

A Guaranteed Method for Failing

It should go without saying that if you want to pass an examination, you should attend it. It sounds stupid, but I mean it. In 1991 in Britain alone, it was estimated that well over 20,000 GCSE candidates failed examinations simply because they didn't turn up!

Sickness is an obvious reason for absence and little can be done about it. 'Nerves' are another reason, but these *can* be kept under your control (see Chapter 6).

The unforgivable reason for absence from exams is not knowing the examination timetable. Make sure you are fully familiar with this – and if you are taking exams set by different examining bodies, make *doubly* sure!

that are found to be 'easy', the effort in preparation for the exams will be correspondingly smaller than for 'difficult' topics, so there is much to be gained by taking as many 'easy' subjects as possible. The problem arises when the 'difficult' subjects are important ones such as English, Mathematics and Science/Technology subjects.

The general rule should be to concentrate sufficiently on the 'important' subjects to give as good a likelihood of success as possible. Then include other 'easy' subjects according to personal interest – but remember that the preparation needed for those extra subjects should not be allowed to affect the time available for the more important ones.

How many subjects should you take? Only you can answer that – unless, of course, the exams are of the 'course' type, in which case the number of exams has already been decided.

▶ Other Demands on Time ◀

This problem relates mostly to part-time students, who may have a full-time job and be studying in the evenings (and/or on day release). These students are likely to be 'mature', and may be married and have children.

The problems here are self-evident and there is no denying the fact that this method of study is infinitely more difficult than being in full-time education. However, the problems can be reduced by using the techniques described in this book.

▶ Late Revision ◀

This is probably the most common cause for alarm. It is a well-known fact that the nearer the examination date approaches, the faster the time seems to disappear! And this is a problem that is unlikely to go away, students being what they are.

The remedy is to have a *routine* for revision. This routine should be initiated as early as possible – at the start of the course, in fact. Once a routine has been in operation for a short time, revision becomes less of a chore and more of a way of life. More details can be found in Chapter 8.

▶ Poor Revision Technique ◀

It is possible to spend a great deal of time on revision and still do badly in examinations. It is another example of 'It's not what you do, it's the way that you do it.'

The advice in this book should help to improve all aspects of preparation for examinations, and Chapter 8 is entirely devoted to revision.

▶ Summary ◀

1. The terms 'pass' and 'fail' refer to a candidate's ability to satisfy examiners' standards or not. They do *not*

refer to a person being a success or failure in any other venture.

2. The 'pass' or 'fail' indicates the candidate's probable ability to (a) enter a course of study, (b) continue with a further section of a course of study, or (c) be considered to be qualified to practice some aspect of a subject studied.

3. The importance of any subject in which a candidate is being examined should be considered carefully. If the subject is an essential one for some qualification, then every effort should be made to give a satisfactory performance in the examination. If the exam is not so important, then consideration should be given to whether it should be taken at all, and whether the time which would have been spent on its revision would not be better spent on other, more important examinations.

4. When the study is part-time and/or when there are other demands on the student's time, it becomes increasingly important to ensure that study is performed in an efficient manner.

Chapter 3

▼

'I can't do this subject'

Our doubts are traitors,
And make us lose the good we oft might win,
By fearing to attempt.

Shakespeare, *Macbeth*

Each one of us, at some time or another, has heard someone say something like 'I was never any good at Maths' or 'I don't like Geography, it's so *boring*.' But it isn't the subject which is at fault, it's the *attitude* of the speaker which is in question.

It is a fact that some subjects appeal to us more than others and we tend to do better at these subjects than the ones we don't like. This is self-evident and hardly needs comment, but we really ought to examine the reasons for our antipathy to certain subjects. All this refers, of course, to subjects which are important to our studies; other subjects can be disliked and ignored without detriment.

Let us consider the statement 'History (or Maths or Geography or whatever) is *boring*.' This just isn't true. No subject, and it is worth stressing, *no subject* is, in itself, boring. It is true that a text book on any subject can be boring (and some are!); the presentation of a subject by some teachers may be boring (no further comment!), but the *subject itself* cannot be dismissed as boring. Let us take an example in an attempt to prove this point.

Suppose two people were asked to describe the first six things which they did every morning. One of them might say something like this: 'Firstly I switch off the alarm; secondly I get out of bed; thirdly I go downstairs – no, wait a minute, I tell a lie – I put my dressing gown on, that's number three; then fourthly I go downstairs; fifthly I feed the cat. Now, what do I do next? I'll think of it in a minute, now let me see . . .' (You are probably bored already so we need go no further.)

The second person may respond with something more like this: 'I rise after switching off the alarm and don my dressing gown before going downstairs to feed the cat (otherwise he'll make my life hell and I'll never be allowed to get my own breakfast). Then . . .'

The important thing is that both of these people are describing *exactly the same series of events*, but one does it in a boring fashion and the other in such a manner that you want to know what he is going to do next.

Academic subjects can be like that. They can be presented in a boring manner, or, if you are lucky, in an interesting way which makes you want to know more. The big problem is that if your early contact with a subject is of the boring type, then your interest runs the risk of being ruined for life. However, if one of these subjects is essential to your studies, then some means of overcoming your aversion must be found, if only for the purpose of making your work for that exam more interesting.

▶ Pet 'Likes' and 'Hates' ◀

At one time, it was generally believed that people were basically either scientifically or artistically orientated. Exceptions to this concept, such as Leonardo da Vinci (who was brilliant in both fields) tended to be ignored as being non-typical and therefore not relevant to an 'ordinary' person. Today, there is some evidence to indicate that every person's brain has potential in both areas, but, if one aspect is exercised more than the other, then the potential which is used less degenerates and becomes

Chemistry is so boring!

During a chance meeting with a mature ex-student, I mentioned that I was considering leaving teaching and going back into industry. He urged me to keep on teaching, if only with a little part-time work. He went on to add, 'You see, I was dreading the thought of the science on the course, especially the Chemistry. At school it was so *boring*. It was just a jumbled mixture of facts. It was different on the course, you made it more like a detective story and it made much more sense. I even borrowed Chemistry books from the library. Earlier, I never thought that I'd do that!'

Interestingly, the Chemistry in the early part of the course was simply a revision of work he'd already done, but in preparation for more advanced work later. So, was it the Chemistry that was boring, or the text books? Or the teaching?

This doesn't apply only to Chemistry. Every subject has been found to be boring by somebody at some time and often it has to do with first impressions. Have you ever taken an instant dislike to a person at a distance, because of his or her appearance? This happens. Often. Have you ever become engaged in conversation with that same person and found that your first impressions were totally wrong and that the person was really quite a likeable character?

If your first impressions about a subject are not favourable, it is very easy to dismiss it as being uninteresting. Try again. If you work at it, you could get a surprise!

overshadowed by that which has been developed to a greater extent. In other words, don't worry if you think that you are 'slow' or 'thick' in one area of study – the

Is it the teacher's fault?

It is easy to claim that teachers are responsible for destroying a pupil's potential interest in a subject. Sometimes this is the case, but not always.

When I was at school, I had a Physics teacher who I felt did not put the subject over well. For a number of reasons I also disliked him as a person and the feeling appeared to be mutual. In my final year, he told me that I should not contemplate a career in anything related to Physics because I would never be any good at it. In my O level exams, my best result was in Physics! Whether I was just being stubborn, saying 'I'll show you', or whether he was a superb psychologist, or both, I'll never know, but it does demonstrate the point.

truth is simply that you haven't had enough practice in your weak subjects!

But let us accept that most people, for whatever reason, tend to fall into a predominantly 'artistic' or 'scientific' category. There is nothing wrong in this, of course. Everyone has the right to pursue whatever interests them most. Parents who insist that their offspring 'follow in Father's footsteps' are ignoring the preferences of the individual child. Later in life many people question the wisdom of their original choice of career (whether they entered it of their own free will or not) and wonder if it is possible to change it.

What is important is that, once your aim has been established (and here I use the word 'aim' to cover interests for more casual study, as well as careers), then individual likes and dislikes within the overall study area need to be identified and acted upon. The 'likes' should present few problems. It's the 'dislikes' that need attention.

▶ Why dislike? ◀

The question to ask yourself is *why* do you dislike a certain subject? The blame cannot always be laid at the door of the teacher or text book – some people find a subject fascinating despite poor text books or even poor teachers. However, such students will not really be perturbed by the sort of dislikes mentioned here. More importantly, many excellent students (and exam candidates) dislike some subjects, so the blame cannot be due to an inherent inadequacy in the student. The reasons for aversions to some subjects must be sought elsewhere.

Disliking a subject is often something of a 'Catch 22' situation. You may dislike a subject because you cannot do it well, and you cannot do it well because you don't like it! The 'chicken and egg' syndrome crops up. Which comes first, the difficulty or the dislike?

The problem goes even further than that. If you don't like a subject, you tend not to work so hard at it, and if you don't work so hard at it, then you become less good at it!

Like any of your faculties, you must *use* it or *lose* it. This applies just as much to playing a musical instrument as to walking. If you practise, you get better, if you don't, you get worse. But one thing is clear. You cannot stand still.

So let us look at the *reasons* why some subjects are less acceptable than others. Think of any subject which you regard as difficult. OK? Now go back to when you *first* studied that subject. How did you get on with the teacher or lecturer? Was he or she good at putting the subject over or did you find yourself at a loss to understand what it was all about?

Perhaps, at first, the subject was OK, but later it became more difficult. What did you do then? What did you do when the subject *started* to become difficult? Did you try harder, or did you (like many thousands of others before

Getting the Right Viewpoint

Three salesmen went into a restaurant for lunch and ordered the chef's special of the day at a cost of £10 per head. The total bill was, therefore, £30. After finishing the meal each gave the waitress a £10 note and she went to the cashier.

'Oh, you've made a mistake' said the cashier, 'there's a special discount of £5 if three meals are ordered at the same table' and she gave the waitress five £1 coins.

The waitress decided that she would make a little profit, so she pocketed two of the £1 coins and returned to the table. She gave each salesman a £1 coin in change, explaining that there had been a small discount.

Each salesman had given £10 and had received £1 change, so each had really paid a total of £9. Three £9s give a total of £27 and the £2 which the waitress took gives a total of £29. What happened to the other £1?

Academic subjects can appear to be as obscure as this, if they are looked at (or presented) from the 'wrong' viewpoint. Try looking at 'difficult' subjects in a different way and they may not seem quite so obscure!

Perhaps you can see through the errors in the logic of this little poser but if, after a concerted try, you can't, the answer can be found on page 34.

you) tend to give up because 'it was too difficult'? Be honest.

When the going got tough, did you (like the tough) get going, or were you not quite so tough and gave up? If we are to progress on this, you must be honest *with yourself.*

Did you really *try* harder? Thousands didn't, and they found that the subject *became* harder. Did you?

I feel sure that, having paused to contemplate this, you will acknowledge that you have neglected your 'pet hate' subject at some time in the past. You should already know what the remedy is. Try again!

▶ Reassessing the Subject ◀

Now, it may be all very well to find where, in the past, you started to stumble over your 'weak subject' (or subjects!). The problem is, how do you rectify this situation? Don't despair. There are several methods.

It all depends upon when you encountered difficulties. If you met them in previous years of whatever course you are taking, then you cannot be *too* bad at the subject, otherwise you would not have been allowed to proceed with your course of study and 'trail' (or resit) a marginally failed exam. If you met the difficulties in *this* year of study, then the problem should be even easier to sort out.

▶ The 'Bracketing' Technique ◀

With this approach, problems with a particular subject can be resolved with comparative ease. All you need to do is go back to your notes and discover where the problems start.

Assuming that the notes refer to the period when your difficulties cropped up, it would be useful to do a quick revision of those notes: but don't worry – I mean 'quick'!

It would be easy to waste a lot of time by going to the beginning of your notes and reading through them from start to finish in an attempt to find the point at which your difficulties began. This is not necessary: there is a simpler way. Go to the *middle* of your notes and read through them. Do they make sense or do you have difficulties? If

Don't leave problems until it's too late

Imagine that you are in a rowing boat and you have lost an oar. You can see that the current is becoming faster and you can hear the roar of a waterfall some distance ahead. You could, of course, do nothing and wait to see what happens, but in so doing you could fail to save yourself.

Alternatively, you could act immediately and try your best to reach the bank of the river and pass the test of how to survive.

Whenever your studies become difficult and you fail to understand the subject material, you *could* do nothing and suffer the consequences later. However, your best chances for academic survival are to act immediately and investigate your problems before they become worse. Once you get too deeply into the problem, getting out of it may require considerably more time than you can spare!

the latter, there is no point in reading on. Go to a point half way between the present position and the beginning (i.e. a quarter of the way through the notes). Read some of that part of the text to ascertain whether or not you understand it. If you do, then the problems arise later in the notes (i.e. between a quarter and a half of the way through); if you don't, then the problem lies earlier still (i.e. between the start and a quarter of the way through). Repeat this bracketing technique until you locate the first point at which you find problems.

Now, it's all very well finding the part of the subject with which you are unhappy, but once you have found it what do you do about it? Once again, there are several techniques which can be brought into use.

▶ Using your Notes ◀

The answer to misunderstandings about certain areas of a subject can sometimes be found in your own notes and there is only one way to find out. Read the notes again!

Go over the material, slowly, taking notice of each point made and try to put each point into the context of the overall subject. Does it make sense? If not, read the notes again, but this time try to number each point and see whether it leads, naturally, to the next. If it does, and you still don't understand, then another method of attack is called for. If it doesn't, then the notes are at fault, at least as far as you are concerned, and this also calls for a different approach.

▶ See the Tutor ◀

The term 'tutor' here refers to tutor, teacher, lecturer or whatever you call the person who was responsible for providing the original subject material.

Very often, when a subject doesn't make sense, a different viewpoint is all that is needed. A good tutor can give you such a viewpoint, providing, of course, that the tutor is available for comment.

Approach the tutor with your problem, specifying the details of the subject with which you are encountering difficulties. It may be that a few words of advice are all that is needed to sort the matter out, in which case your problem is solved. Sometimes further work may be set to introduce you to the subject in a more progressive fashion and to allow you to work the problem out for yourself. Occasionally it could be that your notes are incomplete, for whatever reason, and again this can be corrected with, hopefully, successful results.

OK. So far so good. But what if, for any reason, the tutor is not available? Or the tutor can't 'get the message over'? Maybe the tutor isn't very good (it does happen!), or you simply don't get on with him (or her). Well, we'll have to try a different approach.

▶ **Other Students?** ◀

You can try consulting a fellow student, but this is not such a good idea unless the student *really* understands the subject well. Otherwise it may produce even more confusion. You may be given information which *appears* to be sensible, but is, in fact, misleading or even incorrect. Any misunderstandings which develop at this stage may cause considerable problems later. So, unless you are *absolutely* sure that your colleague can help, it is better to consult a more authoritative source of information.

▶ **The Library** ◀

Most of the information which is given to students comes, originally, from a text book or reference book. Your tutor uses these sources. Consequently, the information which is needed to solve your problem will almost certainly be found in a book or books in your school or college library.

Find a book which deals with your subject and refer to the appropriate chapter and section. Read through this and try to find out about your problem. Some books may present the information in such a way that your difficulty is sorted out fairly easily. You may be lucky and find one of these at the first attempt. The other possibility is that the first book you lay your hands on may be just as obscure as your notes. Don't despair, put it back on the shelf and try another. The answers *are* there. All that you have to do is to find them.

Reference to a suitable book should resolve your problems. However, it must be said that a book which is suitable for one person's needs may be totally unsuitable for another, and maybe *none* of the available books help you. What do you do then?

One missing fact can make all the difference

Could you believe that a *single* fact can make all the difference between something being a problem and being totally understandable? It's true. However, it would be unfair to single out an example from one of the hundreds of examinable subjects, so I'll offer something more general. Consider the following:

Everything had been all right half an hour earlier, when Mandy left the house. She thought it was safe to leave the window open just a few inches, but now she realised how wrong she had been. Little Jason and Kylie lay motionless on a damp patch of carpet. Obviously dead. Suffocated. Although she couldn't prove it, Mandy had a good idea of the identity of the culprit, but she had no intention of phoning for the police.

Most people encountering this story for the first time are puzzled about why a crime was not reported. Some can work it out. Others can't. It's like that with some topics or even full subjects. An understanding of the material can be obscured by a missing fact or principle. Sometimes the relevant detail has been given, but it hasn't 'sunk in'. Occasionally everything makes sense in a flash; other times it takes a long period of maturation in the subconscious before it gels. It all depends on the subject and the person.

Incidentally, the single, critical item omitted from the description above is mentioned on page 35.

▶ The Learning Process ◀

What happens if, after following all this advice, you still can't understand the subject? What you *don't* do is say,

You can lead a horse to water (but it'll only drink if it's thirsty!)

A boy in his early teens was interested in science. He saw little point in fiction and would not give it anything but scant attention. He failed English Literature at O level.

Later, while teaching scientific and technological subjects, he developed an interest in fiction and in writing. He wrote articles on chemical subjects, several short stories and a novel. He wrote dozens of articles on photography and even a book on the subject. Immediately after that, he wrote this book.

It would all have been done more easily, and earlier, had I paid more attention to English Literature at school.

'I'm thick (or 'stupid' or whatever), I'll give it all up.' That will solve nothing.

Assuming that you are qualified to take the course of study (i.e. you have been accepted for the subject because of having passed an earlier year's exam, or for some other valid reason), then you *do* possess the necessary abilities to benefit from the course. This does *not* necessarily mean that you will be able to understand everything in that course – well, not immediately. Everybody has gaps in their understanding, and you are no exception.

An important thing to appreciate is that the process of understanding does not always take place in a smooth and regular fashion. It often happens in definite leaps or jumps. Rather like climbing stairs. You can go up one at a time. Maybe two or even more. But you can't ascend by one and a half, or any other fraction. (Borrowing a term

Where is the missing £1?

The answer to this problem (see page 27), like many academic problems, lies in your viewpoint. Change the way in which you look at the situation and the whole thing takes on a different complexion. Initial attitudes to academic subjects can affect your attitudes for life, but what really matters is whether you are sufficiently interested to try to change any antagonism to a subject.

The way in which this little poser has been presented preconditions most readers into the concept of a total cost of £30. In fact, the cost of the meals is not £30 but £25 – there was a discount of £5. Remember?

Each salesman paid £9, and three times £9 is £27. *Of that* £27, the waitress took £2, and the rest was used to pay for the meal. There is no missing £1!

from Atomic Physics, we could call them 'quantum leaps'.)

Most people have encountered this phenomenon already. You try to understand something which is explained to you (or you read about, or whatever), but it doesn't make any sense. You try again with equal lack of success. But then, some time later, it hits you. 'So *that's* what it's all about! I can't understand why it didn't make sense to me before.' You must have had this experience. Most people have. It is a quantum leap in your understanding.

Another point about those quantum leaps. They are not the same size for each person. They depend upon both the person and the subject. A step in a scientific subject which seems small to a science student may appear enormous to an arts student, and vice versa.

Right then. With all this in mind, it is reasonably safe to say that, sooner or later (and if you keep trying) you *will* understand what is, at the moment, obscure. It is only a matter of time and persistence. Whether or not it happens before the exam is another thing altogether. But remember the point about reaching a satisfactory standard. As long as there are not *too many* blanks in your understanding, then you have little to fear from that exam.

The lesson is, if you don't understand some small detail of a subject after a serious attempt, using the techniques above, then make a comment in your notes and go back to the topic some time later.

▶ Summary ◀

1. No subject is boring. Its presentation may be, but not the subject itself.
2. Most people tend to have an arts or a science bias, but everybody has the potential to be good at both.
3. A subject which is disliked usually receives less attention. The less attention a subject receives, the more

---

Was there a crime?

The police were not called because no crime had been committed. One critical object was omitted from the description on page 32. Had it been mentioned, the event would have been trivial: its omission produced a mini-mystery (for some). The item was Jason and Kylie's home. A goldfish bowl. It had been accidentally knocked off the table by Tom, the family cat, when he jumped in through the open window.

difficult (or boring!) it becomes. You can work to overcome this problem by seeking a different viewpoint.

4. If a subject *becomes* difficult during a period of study, then the cause of the problem should be found as early as possible. Use your notes, your tutor or the library for this.

Chapter 4

▼

The Family Matters

When I was a boy of fourteen, my father was so ignorant I could hardly stand to have the old man around. But when I got to be twenty-one, I was astonished at how much he had learned in seven years.

Mark Twain

The trauma induced by impending examinations does not affect only the student. The rest of the family is almost inevitably drawn into the educational arena. This applies just as much to a parent doing an Open University degree as it does to an offspring preparing for O levels. The rest of the family cannot avoid being involved.

What follows is drawn from real-life situations. None of this is fiction. Family-related problems are so vast that a single book could hardly encompass all of the permutations that exist; for this reason, specific subjects which have been mentioned are used only as examples. Comments on a subject quoted as Law would apply equally to Accountancy or Medicine. Professions or occupations relying on manual dexterity are equally interchangeable, as are references to 'son' or 'daughter' and terms relating to senior members of the family.

▼

My son insists on going out to a disco the night before an exam. I've tried to stop him and tell him that he should stay at home and revise, but he won't listen to me. Is there any argument that I can use to persuade him that he is doing the wrong thing?

You are trying to do the right thing and your intentions are noble, but, on this occasion, your advice is not sound.

Any satisfactory preparation should have been completed long before the eve of the examination. If he hasn't mastered the subject by that time, there is little to be gained by further work at such a late stage. In fact, getting away from the pressures of exams by going out is probably one of the *best* things he could do. 'Letting his hair down' in that way can do him little harm. Most students build up a lot of stress prior to the exams and a period of total, guiltless relaxation can give considerable benefit.

One thing which should not be overlooked, though, is the preparation of the *materials* that he will need for the exams. Pens, a ruler, a calculator and anything else which he will need should be packed away ready for the following day. A last-minute panic on items such as these *will* cause distress so, as long as he is satisfactorily prepared in this way, let him go and enjoy himself. He will have deserved it, and it might promote a good night's sleep.

▼

I am doing the first year of a degree in Law and I hate it. My parents would be absolutely devastated if they knew, so I can't tell them, because my father and my grandfather were both solicitors and Dad expects me to 'follow in his footsteps'. My parents have treated me really well and they have gone to a lot of expense for me, so I just can't disappoint them.

What I want is to be a musician, but they don't understand. I know that what I want to do is very precarious, professionally, and I may never make the grade, but the thought of spending my life dealing with legal matters fills me with dread. I feel that I should be loyal to Dad, but the sacrifice seems too much. What can I do?

You are in a very awkward position. The answer to your problem will be difficult in practice, but, in principle, your way is totally clear. You should not spend your life trying to pay a debt to your parents. You have *your* life to live, and you must live it in the way which suits you. Think about it in this way. Could you do justice to your clients if you practised law (for your parents' benefit) while hating every moment of it? Could you live with *yourself* knowing that you couldn't put in the effort which your clients were entitled to expect of you? You know the answer to this already, so I needn't go on.

For *your* sake, you must make your attitude known to your parents and follow your own interests. If they are fair, they will understand. The alternative is that you may spend the rest of your life resenting the sacrifice which you felt you were obliged to make for their sake.

Before leaving this topic, it might help if I relate a true story about a lady I know very well.

She did extremely well at both O and A level exams and her father was dismayed at her intention to go into catering. He thought that, with her abilities, she had the potential to do much better, so he persuaded her to take up a career in teaching. She spent three years at a teacher training college and a further year teaching in a secondary school. She hated all of it.

She spent the next fifteen years in a variety of jobs in offices, but she never settled in any of them.

Today, she works as a senior cook in a large establishment. She is happy in this role and, given the choice, would never work in an office – or a school – ever again. Need I say more?

▼

My daughter has little interest in school work and is finding it difficult to get down to preparing for her O level exams. She finds studying a bore and can't understand

Confidence Assassination

There is an old saying 'A pinch of praise is worth a pound of criticism' and with the trauma of examinations candidates can use all the confidence boosting they can get. Unfortunately, they are also vulnerable to the reverse effects.

'Grandma, I've passed *eight* O levels!' cried Susan, filled with all the joys of success.

'Rubbish,' Grandma replied, 'they must have made a mistake. Tell them at school tomorrow.'

Young Susan felt demolished. She had been so proud of her accomplishments, but her grandmother had soon put paid to that. It wasn't the first time that such remarks had been made. Nor the last.

This sounds like a piece of fiction, but it is absolutely true. Thirty years later, Susan is still partly recovering from the harm those remarks did. She *ought* not to have worried about it, because four years after the event described she qualified for Mensa with a tested IQ of 160, but despite that she felt she was inferior in some ways.

The moral? When dealing with someone you care about, if you can't say something good, don't say anything. Incidentally, I can vouch for the truth of this story. Susan is my wife.

why all of life can't be more fun. I could pressurise her into taking a more serious attitude to life if she were interested in some sort of career, but she doesn't seem to care about anything except enjoying herself. What can I do?

One of the most frustrating experiences suffered by parents and teachers alike is the knowledge that they can see the younger generation making some of the same mistakes that they did, trying to give advice based on their experiences and having their advice rejected. It is the sort of thing that happens with every generation.

The incentive of a satisfactory career after studying has always been a powerful one, but it only applies to those people who feel seriously about their future. In this case, persuasion based on future job prospects would probably fall on deaf ears. One thing seems certain. Your daughter appears to have no concept of the fact that a satisfactory life consists of variety. A person who works hard for five days each week may dislike the toil involved, but finds weekends are all the more enjoyable because of the contrast. Let her ask any person who has been out of work, and who has little future likelihood of work, whether the prospect of a lifetime of work-free seven-day weeks is 'fun'. She may get a surprise!

If your daughter won't listen to you, is there some other member of your family (or circle of friends) whom she trusts and respects? If such a person can convince her that a normal, happy life consists of a *mixture* of crests and troughs then she may realise that a life of permanent crests is little different from one of permanent troughs. She may also find she gets a certain satisfaction out of the good results that follow hard work!

▼

My daughter wants to be a hairdresser, so she isn't interested in O levels. All that she wants to do is get away from school and start working. How can I persuade her that she should complete her school work first?

This is a common situation. Adolescents often seem reluctant to 'conform', especially to the requirements of 'old' people – i.e. parents or anyone who is more than about twenty years older than themselves. It could well be that your daughter expects to be able to ignore formal education and gain employment at a hairdresser's establishment directly. This may have been acceptable at one time, but not any more.

Career aspirations change with time and the appoint-

ment which appears perfect at first can often become a
*dis*appointment. Hairdressing is no different from many
other occupations in that someone just starting out may
grossly underestimate the type of employment available.
In this case, employment need not be restricted to a local
hairdressing salon. There could be jobs in such widely
different fields as hotels, hospitals or cruise ships, and
additional qualifications – a working knowledge of a
foreign language, say – might be useful. Even if your
daughter's ambition doesn't extend this far at the
moment, most employers expect a qualification *before*
they take on any new staff; others expect them to gain
those qualifications in time. Sometimes an employer is
willing to allow staff time off for study, perhaps one day
per week, but this is not always the case. A full-time
college course first may be a better bet.

For the security of your daughter's future, she should
realise that sooner or later she will *have* to conform to an
employer's requirements, whether she likes it or not. I
would suggest that she gets information from the various
colleges that offer courses in her chosen subject. Entry
requirements are usually good GCSEs (or equivalent) in
English and Mathematics. Sometimes a science subject is
needed, too. Once she realises that this will set her on the
road to her chosen career, she may develop a sudden
interest in school work!

▼

*I have been doing well during the first year of my degree
course and my problem is not so much the examinations
which are approaching as those in future years. I got
married a few months ago and my husband is very
traditional in his ideas. He is not very happy about my
doing a degree and thinks that I should be constantly by
his side. At the moment he works in a factory but hates it
and he wants us to have our own business.*

*My problem is, should I give up my studies for his sake,
or should I continue to study, even though I know that it
will cause friction in the family?*

It is always difficult when you have divided loyalties. On the one hand, you want to make a good start to your married life and have a harmonious relationship with your husband. On the other, you know that, with hard work, you are likely to be able to gain a degree and satisfy your own interests in life, even though, initially, your husband may have to make a few sacrifices on your behalf.

If you cast your mind back to when you started the course, you will probably realise that an academic year is not such a long time. It can pass very quickly indeed. The next two years will pass just as quickly. If, at the end of that short period, you get your degree, it will be with you for life, and nobody can take it away. If you spend those two years (and how many more?) starting up a business with your husband, you have to look at other sides of the question. Will you be happy doing it? Will the business succeed? If it doesn't succeed, or if it does but you are not happy with that type of life, what happens then? You cannot guarantee that you will be able to take up your degree course again. You may not even want to. Think also that you may go through the rest of your life regretting not having obtained a qualification when you had the opportunity.

Naturally, a serious discussion with your husband is going to be needed, but if he is prepared to give and take, as you seem to be, he should agree that the best course of action for all concerned is for you to finish your studies. After that you can experiment with your career – and your new business – as much as you like without losing the one thing that you are aiming for at the moment.

▼

My son suffers from asthma and I think that the stress of exams brings on the attacks. The last time he was waiting to go into the examination room, he had such a bad attack that he had to go to hospital. Is there anything that can be done?

It would be inappropriate for me to comment on medical conditions. The best authority on that is your doctor or a specialist. But the root of your son's problems may be the stressful nature of the exams and the preparation for them. That stress can be tackled and if, as you say, it is stress that brings on the attacks, then I may be able to be of some help.

The first point to be appreciated is that it is often the *fear* of failure, rather than failure itself, that causes stress and it is this fear that should be tackled initially. It has been mentioned elsewhere in this book that failing an exam should not be regarded as an earth-shattering experience. The prospect of failure should not be allowed to cause stress. If the worst happens, candidates often have the chance to resit, possibly after repeating part or all of the course. Secondly, as long as the candidate has had an adequate background in the subject being examined and has prepared properly for the exam, the possibility of failure should not be entertained. The advice in this book should see to that.

However, there is one other thing that is often overlooked. Anxiety is infectious and the fear of not living up to *other people's* expectations can cause as much stress as the exams themselves. As a parent, you should be honest with yourself here – are you putting pressure on your son to achieve more than he is capable of? Or are his teachers pushing him too hard?

On a more positive note, the relaxation exercises given in Appendix 4 should help your son to reduce the effect of his reactions to the sort of stress associated with examinations. Benefit from these exercises is slow. It takes practice to be able to relax properly, but if initial responses seem promising, then further efforts are likely to be even more so.

▼

My mother is in her late eighties and we can't leave her on her own. When we go out, we ask our son to stay in to do his revision so that he can keep an eye on her. She is no trouble and all she wants to do is watch television but he objects, saying that he can't revise. He's only got to read, so I think he's just being awkward. Don't you think I'm right?

As you've asked for my opinion, I will say no, I think you're wrong. If he wanted to read a magazine or do something which didn't demand too much of his attention, then OK, but revision for exams is another thing altogether. He needs to concentrate on the work in hand and he can't do that with the television vying for his attention or with the risk of interruption if his grandmother *does* need something. Studying can only be done properly with uninterrupted peace and quiet, away from the temptations of television.

Why not try to compromise? If he could revise in a different room, well away from distractions, then both aims could be achieved. He could call in to see his grandmother every half hour or so, whenever he needed a short break from his studies, and you could go out with an easy conscience.

▼

My son is at university and he tells me that he has done practically no work during his first year. It is now two weeks before his exams and he is worried because he hasn't started revising yet. What advice can I give him?

If I knew of a method for condensing a full year's university-level work into two weeks, I could start an expensive correspondence course and become very wealthy. To be serious, though, I wouldn't say much for the value of any degree that could be obtained by such an approach.

Your son has cause to be worried. He is in an impossible situation and there is no help that anyone can give him which will guarantee success in his examinations.

You don't mention whether his year's practical and/or set work is up to standard, but from what you say I assume not. This in itself will put him at a disadvantage with the examination board. As far as his examinations are concerned, he has two lines of action open to him. Firstly, he can cram as much as possible into the time left and try to tackle every exam. I would say that his chances were very slender, though. His second option is to concentrate on one or two exams and try to do well in these. His chances of success would be rather higher, but they still won't be great. In any event, he should obtain advice from his tutor about the regulations concerning course work and examination requirements, because he may be wasting his time with a last-minute effort.

I'm sorry that I can't be more helpful than this, but your question is not much different from asking how you can give him twenty-five years of your practical experience of life overnight. And you know the answer to that!

▼

My daughter is obsessed with studying for her exams. Every night after dinner she goes into her room and revises for four or five hours at a time. Sometimes she even reads well into the early hours. She does this seven days a week. Surely it is too much?

It is indeed. What she is doing is excessive and probably not very efficient either. The brain can take in only so much information in any single session and a session lasting about thirty to forty-five minutes should be just about right. Anything longer than this will probably result in wasted effort. More information about subdividing revision can be found in Chapter 8.

Students who try to revise for such long periods tend to do it because they feel guilty if they don't study for all of the time available. They work on the assumption that the more effort they put in, the more benefit they get from it. It doesn't quite work that way, but it is not easy to get this message over.

One way in which this may be achieved is by asking her whether she gets as much benefit from a double period of some subject, or whether two, separate, 'normal' periods are better. If she is honest, she will admit that, by the end of a double period, she is pretty well saturated or, more likely, *over*saturated. If this observation is translated into her private study, then she should be able to realise that very long periods of study are not a good thing.

One other point is that studying should be interspersed with periods of self-assessment (*see* Chapter 9), as this gives some measure of relief from intense study. Nevertheless, after, say, a couple of hours of varied study, it is a good idea to have a complete break, if only for fifteen minutes or so. Considerable benefit from this is virtually guaranteed.

▼

How can I make my son revise for his O level exams? He says that he really wants to, but he never quite gets around to it. I'm frightened that if he leaves his revision much later, he won't have enough time to do all the work needed.

Let me take your points in reverse order. Yes, your comment about leaving revision until too late is perfectly sound. Last-minute 'cramming' is not likely to do a great deal of good. A less concentrated effort over a longer period of time will be of much more benefit.

The comment that he 'really wants to' is, of course, simply not true. If he wanted to get down to revision, he would do so. What he means is that he knows that he *ought* to get down to revision, but he can't quite bring himself around to doing it.

Now, to go back to your original question. The simple answer is 'You can't!' Nothing you can do will *make* your son revise. You can only advise or encourage him to do what is needed. If his revision is to be done satisfactorily, he must do it of his own volition. The problem here is his lack of *motivation*. There are dozens of possible reasons for this. Have you encouraged him to study? Can he work at home without distractions? Is he interested in his subject(s)? (If not, you could try the 'new viewpoint' approach discussed in Chapter 3.)

However, you must remember that many students, and especially those without a satisfactory technique, find revising for exams very daunting. The important thing is not to try to force him to revise, but rather to find out why he will not do so, and then take steps accordingly.

▼

How can we help our son with his revision? My wife's offers seem to be rejected automatically and I have very limited knowledge of the subjects with which he seems to be having difficulty. Somehow we seem to be letting him down. What can we do?

There seem to be two problems here. For some reason, your wife's offers appear to be unwelcome. A good parent could be described as one who is always available without always being present, and this may apply in your wife's case. There isn't a great deal she can do about this, apart from being 'available'. If she makes it clear that she is there to be asked, but leaves it to your son to do the asking when *he* wants to, the situation may improve in time.

Reading between the lines, it appears that you don't have this difficulty, so why not offer yourself as assistant with your son's self-assessment? There is no reason to be troubled because you don't know much about a particular subject. Parents can't be well informed on *everything*. After all, even teachers tend to specialise!

For the subjects with which you are unfamiliar, you could use your son's notes on a given topic and ask him questions about it. If appropriate, ask him to quote a definition, then explain to you what it means. This is one of the best ways of testing a person's understanding. Act dumb, especially if he appears to be quoting the notes parrot fashion rather than *explaining* what the subject is about. Weak spots in understanding will soon reveal themselves when this technique is used. If it's a subject you know nothing about, this could even be an advantage – he'll *have* to explain it clearly to make you understand, and this will help him clarify his own thoughts.

Perhaps, with a tactful approach, on occasions when you may not be in a position to help, your wife could take over your role? It can't do any harm and, who knows, it may get over the initial problem.

If for academic reasons – if he's studying Technology at a more advanced level than you or your wife ever did, for example – you are unable to help directly, you could encourage him to team up with a fellow student and use the techniques we have been discussing. Although, as we saw in Chapter 2, he should be. wary of taking a colleague's opinion as gospel, this can be a good way for both students to help each other and to identify any gaps in their knowledge and understanding. (We'll look at this subject in more detail in Chapter 9.)

▼

We were happy when my wife had a part-time job, but a few years ago, when we needed a second car, she went full time. Since then, in order to get qualifications for promotion, she has started studying in the evenings. Now this educational thing seems to have taken over. We hardly see her. My meals are ready when I come home from work, but after that she's off studying. It strikes me that she is more interested in her studies than her family. I don't think it's fair. I have an executive position and earn enough money for all our needs, so I think that she should give up work and look after me and the boys. Don't you agree?

She can't win, can she? When you needed another car, you were quite happy for her to take on the responsibilities of a full-time job, in addition to being a housewife and mother. Have you considered that now she might be interested in the career itself, not just the money.

All of us need some sort of challenge in life. Obviously, your wife is serious about making progress in her job: working full time and studying as well is by no means easy. What she needs is help and you are the best person to give it to her. Have you considered how you felt when you were struggling to get to the position that you are in now? She probably feels the same. After all, the whole family is going to benefit in the long run, so why not try to encourage her in her studies and give assistance when she needs it, such as before examinations? She could resent it, if you don't.

▶ Summary ◀

1. Every member of the family is affected when one of them is preparing for examinations. Each one should make allowances for these unusual circumstances.
2. Family members who wish to help should be 'available', but should not attempt to force their assistance on the exam candidate.
3. Exam candidates need a suitable environment in order to study and this may mean the rest of the family making some sacrifices, albeit on a temporary basis. A quiet, distraction-free environment is essential for satisfactory study.
4. The only person who can do the *work* for the exams is the candidate, but motivation can involve the whole family. Encouragement may be needed, but the threat of 'punishment' for failure is rarely, if ever, successful.
5. Basic literacy and numeracy, and sometimes specialist knowledge or practical skills, are a prerequisite for entry into most courses for higher study – and for employment.
6. 'Advice' on career matters should be based on the interests of the *student*, not the family. It can be frustrating to spend a working lifetime climbing to the top of the professional ladder only to find that it has been placed against the wrong building!

Chapter 5

▼

Health and the Studying Environment

The best thinking has been done in solitude. The worst has been done in turmoil.

Thomas Alva Edison

▶ Where do I study? ◀

A student's accommodation can have a profound effect on the efficiency of study, and accommodation varies widely in terms of both convenience and suitability. However, one problem which is common to virtually every situation is that of external noise. There is nothing much you can do about traffic noise or overhead aircraft apart from moving to somewhere quieter, but you can take steps to avoid other distractions.

A student living in a hall of residence may appear to have the ideal accommodation, but these places are not always as quiet as you might like. Libraries are the obvious alternative choice for study (for all kinds of student), as they offer not only the necessary quietness, but also a comfortable environment in which to work. The presence of others working in the same way is also a bonus, psychologically. Libraries, however, have to close – often just when you are getting into your swing with your studies.

Working in lodgings or at home is different. You may be disturbed by the sound of televisions, radios or audio equipment, not only from within your own building, but also from the immediate neighbourhood. While it is true that you can work to ignore such sounds, it still requires an effort to do so, and with serious studies the brain's activities should be centred on the task in hand. Many students claim that background music helps them to work. This may or may not be true, but my reaction is to ask have you *ever* tried to work without such sounds? You may be surprised at the improvement in your concentration.

Distractions from friends or family can be countered by adhering strictly to a specific working timetable and permitting no interruptions whatsoever. Friends soon 'get the message' if you are adamant on this point. You can put genuine friendship to good use by arranging for them to come around for a chat, or whatever, at a specific time *after* your predetermined period of study. At such a time their company should contribute to your relaxation and escape from intense academic concentration. After all, the chances are that a number of your friends have exams at the same time, so you should be able to help and support each other.

If you are working at home and you don't have a study room of your own, then there can be substantial problems. Your need for a quiet and peaceful environment without distractions may well be incompatible with the requirements of the rest of your family. The other members of your household will need to be understanding about your needs, while you may have to make compromises too. Try to find a room where you can be undisturbed at specific times without upsetting the family routine. Use the bedroom you share with a brother or sister while he/she is watching television or out; the kitchen after the evening's cooking and washing up are done; the dining room when everyone else has moved through to the lounge. If you really can't work in peace and quiet at home, ask a friend if you can study at his house.

▶ **Health Factors** ◀

The very process of studying often overshadows thoughts about personal health and the environment in which the studying takes place. This may be understandable, but don't forget that a healthy and active mind requires a healthy and active body. It also requires a healthy environment in which to study.

Advice on these matters can vary widely, some 'experts' claiming that physical health must take priority over all else while others insist that the brain requires the greater attention. Neither is totally right, nor totally wrong – it all depends upon the individual in question. What *is* true is that, all too often, student ailments, with their adverse effects on academic performance, result from ignorance of these matters and/or lack of control of them. For obvious reasons, students who live away from home are particularly susceptible. But there are a few essentials which apply to everybody and which we can consider here.

▶ **Exercise** ◀

Exercise helps to maintain a healthy body and mind, but it must be regular. For example, it is pointless, if not dangerous, to jog for one hour once a month. A *daily* exercise lasting a fraction of this time would be far more beneficial. If you are naturally sedentary, try to take up some physical activity such as cycling, swimming or dancing. If this is not practical, then walking, rather than taking the bus (if only for a part of the journey) is better than no exercise at all. Whatever physical activity you choose, it should not be taken as a duty. Do it because you *enjoy* it. In this way you gain a double benefit.

There is evidence to show that regular exercise reduces the risk of coronary heart disease, increases general health and improves other faculties such as eyesight, hearing and powers of observation. Exercise on its own is unlikely to help you to lose weight, but it could well contribute to your not gaining it, especially later in life!

▶ Diet ◀

Students are not alone in neglecting the value of the food they eat. Healthy eating is often thought to be inconvenient or too expensive. Convenience and take-away foods are often highly processed, with much of the valuable content destroyed. They tend to be rich in 'unhealthy' components such as saturated fats, sugar, salt and synthetic additives incorporated more for the sake of cost, appearance or shelf-life, than for the benefit of the consumer.

There is already enough publicity concerning the bases of 'healthy' diets to render repetition here unnecessary, but variety in content is probably the best abbreviation of the general message. Hence, a 'healthy' diet is one that consists of a suitable *balance* of proteins, carbohydrates, fats, vitamins, minerals and trace elements.

Even if you have a healthy diet, you can cancel out its benefits by inappropriate eating habits, at least as far as studying is concerned. Heavy, cooked meals, requiring much effort on the part of the digestive system, tend to bring on a feeling of drowsiness. This is especially true if the meal is accompanied by alcohol. Hence, prior to a period of study, a light meal, such as a salad, would be more appropriate. Equally, before a morning examination, a breakfast of cereal or fruit would be preferable to a full cooked 'English breakfast'.

▶ Alcohol ◀

Despite claims by many drinkers to the contrary, the consumption of alcohol does *not* improve the performance of any activity. What it *does* do is to depress the activity of all functions, including all aspects of judgement. There is ample scientific evidence to show that the consumption of alcohol has a detrimental effect on the ability to perform even the simplest mathematical calculations, so there can be no doubt that more complex academic studies will also be affected adversely. Don't drink before or during a serious period of study, and don't drink just before an exam: you will not perform to the best of your ability if you are even mildly 'under the influence'.

▶ Sleep ◀

The amount of sleep an individual needs decreases with age, but most adults require something in the order of eight hours' sleep a night if its natural benefits are to be maximised. However, immediately prior to examinations, sleep can often be elusive. This is hardly surprising under the circumstances.

The occasional loss of a full measure of sleep appears to do little harm, but a sustained loss is known to have an adverse effect on academic activities and concentration.

In addition to the self-evident matter of personal comfort in bed – including establishing the temperature that suits you and maintaining adequate ventilation, which we will discuss shortly – factors that can affect sleep include consumption, before retiring, of large amounts of food (with the possibility of associated indigestion) or excessive quantities of beverages which contain caffeine, such as tea or coffee. Have a warm milky drink or herbal tea last thing at night instead.

Minimising worry can be assisted by not studying immediately before bedtime. Spending half an hour watching television, listening to music or reading non-academic material will help you relax and increase the likelihood of untroubled sleep. Gentle exercise, such as a late-night walk, also helps.

Some exercises which facilitate relaxation and sleep are described in Appendix 4.

▶ **Heating and Ventilation** ◀

If you have lived in poorly heated 'digs' you will be well aware of the problems involved with low temperatures. But temperatures which are too high can also have an adverse effect on studies. Centrally heated study rooms, including libraries, are often too warm, inducing some measure of drowsiness. Electric heating is convenient and easily controllable but it is expensive compared with other forms of heating.

Both central heating and electric heating have the disadvantage of lowering the relative humidity of the atmosphere. This results in the air feeling 'dry' and can produce some discomfort in the form of dryness of the nose and throat and the associated increased thirst.

The burning of fossil fuels (coal, oil, paraffin and gas) is a cheaper form of heating and one of the products of such combustion is water vapour. This tends to offset the 'dryness' produced by the types of heating mentioned above, that is, if the products of combustion are allowed to escape into the room. However, there can be certain disadvantages, and we will deal with them in a moment.

As a general rule, for the purpose of study, it is preferable to be warmly dressed in a room with a temperature which is slightly lower than the 'ideal comfort' level.

Most people take the composition of the atmosphere completely for granted and it is only when large numbers of people are crowded in an enclosed space (especially a warm one) that the importance of ventilation and 'quality' of air becomes forcefully apparent!

In many ways, the requirements of the human body are similar to those of the internal combustion engine. It needs both fuel (food), and oxygen in order to burn that fuel. The product of that human 'combustion' is the energy essential for all of the normal functions of the body. Most people understand this principle. What is not so well known is that the brain uses rarely less than 20 per cent, and sometimes as much as 50 per cent of the body's total oxygen intake. So, even when you are sitting down studying (and not engaged in physical exercise), your brain still needs a considerable amount of oxygen.

There is no problem with this oxygen demand out of doors, nor, for that matter, indoors when there is ample ventilation. But problems can arise when you are studying in a room with insufficient supply and circulation of fresh air. This applies whenever a room is treated so as to minimise draughts – a common occurrence in cold weather. What happens under such circumstances is that, as a result of normal respiration, the oxygen content of the air is depleted and is replaced by increasing concentrations of carbon dioxide and water vapour, the by-products of the 'combustion' process mentioned above. The smaller the room, the faster this process takes place. The resulting symptoms include being too warm, the air seeming damp, a dry feeling in the nose and throat and some discomfort in breathing. There may also be a tendency to headaches. All this indicates that the brain is finding it increasingly difficult to acquire sufficient oxygen.

The cure for this is obvious. Stop studying for a while and get some fresh air. Also, get some fresh air into the room – even if it means a drop in temperature. A break from mental work, under these circumstances, will be a definite advantage.

The potential problems associated with a lack of adequate ventilation can become considerably more serious if heating is achieved by combustion processes, i.e. by burning coal, liquid fuels or gas. Adequate ventilation of the appliance is *absolutely essential*, for several reasons. You and the heating appliance will be competing for a limited and ever-decreasing supply of oxygen. To counter this possible problem, it is necessary to ensure that the heating appliance receives an adequate supply of air, even if this means having to tolerate draughts.

It should be obvious that the byproducts of the combustion should not be allowed to accumulate in the study room, if at all possible, as these will contribute to the 'stuffiness'. In this respect, you will have little control with portable gas heaters, but with open fires, fitted gas fires and central heating boilers a flue is an integral part of the system. However, this does not mean that there are no dangers with such systems as the flue *must* function efficiently, otherwise the byproducts may escape into the room. This can happen if the flue is damaged or, in the case of open fires, if the flue passage has excessive deposits of soot.

The effects of an accumulation of the byproducts of combustion in the study room have already been described, but there is a further hazard. With all forms of combustion, the nature of the byproducts depends upon the amount of oxygen available for combustion. If this is restricted *in any way*, then, in addition to carbon dioxide, carbon monoxide may be produced. This is particularly dangerous. Not only is it extremely poisonous, but it is colourless, tasteless and odourless, so it cannot be identified by any of the senses. In the absence of specialised equipment it can only be detected by the symptoms which it produces. Early indications include drowsiness, mental confusion, redness of the skin and headaches. If most or all of these symptoms are experienced *only* when the heating appliance is used and also *every time* it is used, then a check on the heating system is imperative because one of the next symptoms of carbon monoxide poisoning is unconsciousness. Does any more need to be said?

▶ Lighting ◀

This is another aspect of the study environment which is frequently neglected. Satisfactory lighting is essential. It minimises the risk of eye strain (which can also lead to headaches) and increases the efficiency of your studying.

Man's eyes have been evolving in natural light for millions of years, while electric lighting has been with us for only a microscopic fraction of that time. It is not surprising, therefore, that natural daylight is the best form of illumination under which to study. However, this is not

you want it. Once the picture is in your mind, you will never forget the planets and their order.

▼

That sounds like a good technique and I'm sure that the picture will stay in my memory but I could confuse the 'M' of the Mercury with the 'M' of Mars.

Not really. Mercury is nearest to the sun. Therefore it will be very hot. So hot, in fact, that metals will be molten – and most people know that mercury is liquid at room temperature. The first 'M' is, therefore Mercury and the second (which is nearer to the 'military') must represent Mars. Confusion avoided? You can make similar 'subsidiary mnemonics' to suit all sorts of lists you need to memorise.

▼

Yes. But now I have another question. When I was small, I remembered lots of things by reciting rhymes. It seems childish now, but the method did work. What have you got to say about that?

I don't see anything wrong with it. The important thing is that you should use *any* technique which works for you. In fact, you may be surprised at the number of people who remember the days of the month by reciting:

Thirty days hath September,
April, June and November

and so on. It doesn't matter what mnemonic you use, as long as it does the job it's supposed to do.

Perhaps I didn't stress this enough earlier, but the best mnemonic is the one that you invent for yourself. The basis is that, if you can produce a mnemonic for yourself at some time or other, then you can do it again later. After

all, if you actually *invented* the system, then you won't
have to rely on memory to recall it because it is *yours*!

▼

*OK, that will work for all sorts of lists. But what about
dates?*

Dates can be a problem, but there are still tricks that can
be employed. By way of example, let us take Christopher
Columbus's discovery of America. Memorising that particular date uses what is probably the most common
mnemonic of all. I'm sure you know the one I mean:

In fourteen hundred and ninety-two
Columbus sailed the ocean blue.

This seems to be a sure way of remembering dates, but
there can be problems. Let me give you an example of
what I mean.

Most people, at some time or another, have left home
and wondered about something like 'Did I switch the
cooker off?' or 'Did I lock the front door?' The more they
think about the omission, the more they convince themselves that they *did* forget some important detail. And this
is under *normal* circumstances. Under examination conditions, your doubts may be infinitely more intense. So
what do you do about it? The answer is to have a back-up
mnemonic.

Take the Columbus example again. Under examination conditions, you could ask yourself, 'Was it *fourteen*
hundred and ninety-two? Could it have been *thirteen*
hundred and ninety-two?' The metre, or poetic rhythm, is
the same, so you could be mistaken. Similarly, could it
have been 'eighty-two' rather than 'ninety-two'? The
more you doubt, the more convinced you can become
that you are wrong. Furthermore, the concept of 'bone',
'door', 'mine' and 'shoe' doesn't really help much.

Here's a suggestion. In 1492, Columbus sailed to
America. Today many Americans cross the Atlantic the
other way to visit Europe. It is 'A Trip Americans Do'. 'So

what?' you may ask. Count the letters of each of the words in the statement and you'll come up with 1, 4, 9, 2. No mistakes there! You can do something similar for other dates you may need to remember. Furthermore, this method can be used for other numbers as well as dates – telephone numbers for example. Naturally, remembering telephone numbers won't help with exams, but the more you practise this method, the more proficient you will become – and the more applications you will find for its use.

▼

That is a useful tip. Now I understand what you meant when you talked about referencing my mental card-index system. It's all a matter of imagination and application.

Another thing I'm weak on is names of places. Capital cities and that sort of thing. What sort of advice would you give for that?

That's quite an easy one, really. The method is to keep the names together, rather than separate. We do this sort of thing all the time, so all we have to do is repeat the process consciously. Let me explain.

If I were to ask you how many people you knew with the name 'Albert' you might take quite some time to think of all the men you know, or have heard of, with the first name Albert. You would attach their family names after-wards. On the other hand, *some* Alberts might come complete with surnames. Albert Einstein could be an example. If his name cropped up, in all probability you didn't think of him as an Albert who had the family name of Einstein. You remembered the name as a coherent whole: 'Alberteinstein'. Similar considerations would apply to 'Henrytheeighth' (not the eighth member of a series of Henrys, but a unit in his own right). Michaeljackson and Maggiethatcher could form the start of a list to which, no doubt, you will be able to add further examples of your own.

So, when you think of capital cities, don't say, 'What is

the capital of the state of Colorado, or the country Colombia?' Instead, think of 'Denvercolorado' or 'Bogotacolombia'. Once you have recorded facts in your memory in this way, the answers to the questions above emerge automatically. You will not need to think about them.

▼

You're right. I do think of names in the way you describe and I have remembered some places, like towns in counties, in that way. I just didn't think of using it as a general memory aid.

Another thing. So far, you have described a number of different techniques for different circumstances. What bothers me now is that it looks as if I am going to need a new mnemonic for each memory problem that crops up. I don't feel too happy about that.

Your feelings are quite natural, but there is no need to get dismayed about this. Dealing with the subject of memory more fully would take a full book in its own right, but this is not necessary in your case. What we have been looking at here is a means of assistance, not another subject to be studied. You have been given enough examples to cover virtually all the requirements which you may have. Now it is up to you to exploit the techniques and, more importantly, to expand their applications. Let me give one final example.

The process of running names together, as described above, can be extended to help in all sorts of areas of study. For example, in Chemistry, many students find difficulties with the Periodic Table, trying to remember the order in which the elements occur. There should be no problem. Believe it or not, the last mnemonic discussed will sort it out for you.

The Periodic Table is an arrangement of the elements, listed in increasing order of atomic number and structured in such a way that the elements fall into vertical groups having similar, predictable properties. If you can remember the first eighteen elements in order, then the upper structure of the table follows almost automatically and details of the vertical columns can be filled in when required. For example, the alkali metals, also remembered in order, can be placed in the first vertical column, under lithium and sodium. Similarly, the halogens can be placed under fluorine and chlorine. The problem lies in remembering the first eighteen elements.

The first nine elements are hydrogen (H), helium (He), lithium (Li), beryllium (Be), boron (B), carbon (C), nitrogen (N), oxygen (O) and fluorine (F).

Hydrogen tends to stand apart, almost as an isolated element in its own right and to a certain extent, helium is treated in the same way. Hence seven vertical columns of elements are headed by lithium at one end and fluorine at the other. The tenth element, neon, goes at the head of the eighth vertical column, but, for the sake of the mnemonic (and *only* for the sake of the mnemonic), we will place it in the next set of eight elements. These are Neon (Ne), sodium (Na), magnesium (Mg), aluminium (Al), silicon (Si), phosphorus (P), sulphur (S) and chlorine (Cl).

Now let me introduce you to the chemists' periodic friends Eli and Nina. Eli has a peculiar surname, but it is worth remembering. It is 'Bebcnof'. In fact, we have been a little unfair to Eli in that we have been rather remiss in pronouncing his name. It should begin with an H – or, more accurately, a double H. His name, therefore, is Hheli Bebcnof or, to put it in more scientific terms H He Li Be B C N O F. The first nine elements in their correct order!

Nina's name has been misspelt. I suppose that you can guess the correct one. Yes, Nena. The surname is a double-barrelled one, Mgalsi-Pscla. It is difficult to pronounce, but it is worth the effort. Nena Mgalsi-Pscla gives us Ne Na Mg Al Si P S Cl A, the second series of elements in their correct order!

Remember those two names and you'll never have problems with this topic.

Memory, Revision and Self-Assessment

In Chapter 9, the use of index cards is advocated as an abbreviated form of self-examination: I explain that, once amended, these can also double up as a form of revision. A similar principle can be employed as a mnemonic.

Imagine a set of index cards containing condensed details of a subject on which you are to be examined. Instead of storing these in a box, imagine them being arranged on a large sheet of paper covering a table. Imagine that the *title* of the subject, in bold characters, is placed in the centre. The next step is to select a topic within the total subject which can be considered a mini-subject in its own right, that is, a topic which could form the basis of a full examination question. If you were studying Shakespeare, say, a topic within the subject might be 'the tragedies'. Place the first card which deals with this topic immediately above the title card, followed by the next card, and so on. There could be sub-topics which do not form a coherent part of the main one – other dramatists of the Shakespearian period, perhaps – in which case arrange them on side paths rather like the branches of a tree. In your mind's eye, link any side branches, or even 'twigs', together with pen or pencil lines, with any appropriate explanatory notes.

Repeat this process with each of the other topics to produce 'trees' radiating outwards from the central title. Any links between the twigs of one tree and any other (i.e. related matters in different topics within the same overall subject) should be marked and, if necessary, commented upon.

After this imaginary process has been completed, you will have a full examinable subject spread out on the table in an abbreviated and linked format. A whole year's subject, before you, at a glance, with related items connected with guidelines!

This is not mere imagination. It can be used as a means of memorising an entire subject – or many subjects, for that matter. Full details of this technique is beyond the scope of this book, but a look at the general principles could be useful.

In this chapter, emphasis has been placed on the use of visual images as a means of assisting the memory. Any method of achieving this visual imagery is valid as long as it works for you. Instead of using index cards, try performing the exercise described above with brief, boxed comments. Use any means to stress points of interest – imagine different shaped boxes, different colours (similar colours linking similar sub-topics) – in fact *anything* that will assist in making a dramatic, visual image.

Once you have done this, you will have a picture of the full subject, together with visual mnemonics, ready to be stored in your memory. It may sound complicated, but try it. You are likely to find it a lot easier to practise than it is to describe!

▼

You make it sound so easy. But you have picked out some specific examples which, I'll bet, are the easiest to remember. Am I correct?

No, not at all. With the shopping list, you can use *any* list of items which you choose. Try it and see. Choose the most difficult list that you can imagine and the system will still work. (Incidentally, if you don't like the word 'bone' for number 1, substitute it with 'gun' – or, for that matter any word that will serve to remind you of the number 1.) Similarly, the last example is possibly one of the most difficult lists of names to remember, but the mnemonic still works. What is important is not so much the examples which I have given, but the mnemonics which *you* design for yourself. Use your imagination, invent your own mnemonics and you will *never* forget them!

▶ Summary ◀

1. Don't assume that memory is all you need for examinations. Understanding is also required and the amount of understanding increases with increasing academic level.
2. At any level, try to *understand* as much as possible. What cannot be understood will need to be committed to memory.
3. Interest in a subject enhances the efficiency of memory.
4. Memorising facts is only half the battle. *Recall* is just as important, if not more so.
5. Mental pictures are easier to remember than abstract concepts. The more outstanding (or outrageous) the mental images, the more likely they are to be remembered.
6. Rhymes may seem childish as mnemonics, but if they work, then use them.
7. Running words together aids associations between words and sometimes symbols.
8. The best mnemonics are home-made. They are the ones you are least likely to forget.

Chapter 8

▼

Revision

It is not enough to be busy . . . the question is:
what are we busy about?
Henry David Thoreau

Revision is one of the most daunting processes involved in the examination system. A great deal of time can be spent (and sometimes wasted) in revision, but, as with every other activity, there are good methods and bad methods for revision. The techniques described here show how to minimise the time spent on, and maximise the efficiency of, the revision process.

▼

When I put my year's notes on the table and look at the amount of work I have to get through, I get depressed and feel like giving up. It makes me feel sick, and, often enough, I just put the revision off until another time.

I'm not surprised. But what makes you think that you are different from other examination candidates? Most of those who start off in that way feel pretty much the same. Your problem is that you are using a bad technique. Let me use an illustration to try to show you where you are going wrong.

Imagine that you have been invited to one of those medieval banquets – you know, the ones where guests are treated to seven or eight courses over the duration of the night. What would be your reaction if you were invited to put an entire plateful of food in your mouth in

one go? Even worse, what about tackling the entire seven
or eight courses in one go? Yes, it is absurd, and yes, it
very well could make you feel sick at the mere thought of
it.

When you stare at a whole year's notes (or, even
worse, those for a whole course), you are doing the same
thing. Your brain also has a limit to the amount of material
with which it can cope in any given period of time, so
don't give yourself mental indigestion.

▼

That's all very well for you to say, but I've still got to get
through all that work haven't I? Technique won't change
any of that.

Correct. As you say, technique won't diminish the
amount of work which you need to do, but it will change
your *attitude* to it, because that is where your major
problem lies. Incidentally, a revision timetable will help
(see the box opposite for suggestions).

Getting back to your banquet. When the first course is
presented, there are no problems. You can enjoy tucking
into that, but, notice, *at your leisure*. You take your time
and eat the food at a pace that suits you, and without a
thought for the next course. In other words, you take the
meal in small, *easily managed* portions.

Your revision should be taken in pretty much the same
way. Forget about the overall mass of work that needs to
be done. Instead, nibble away at it in small, easily
digested portions.

▼

So, are you saying that I should take the revision in one-
page portions or do you mean that I should split the
whole year's work into seven or eight parts?

No, not exactly. What I am saying is that you should split
the year's work into *suitable* portions. The word 'suitable'
needs to be clarified, though.

Firstly, you should already have a syllabus for the

Organise a revision timetable

A well-organised approach, adhering to a strict timetable, makes revision easier. It is also less time-consuming than a haphazard approach. The following timetable is recommended, but may need to be modified depending on your circumstances.

During the course
Course work should be revised on a regular basis, ideally every day.

Eight to ten weeks before the exams
The entire course work should be scanned superficially and divided into easily assimilated packages.

Six to eight weeks before the exams
Serious revision should commence.

The evening before the exam
All work should have been completed. No new revision should be done.

year's work. If you haven't, get one. (Naturally, if the exam is a final one covering more than a single year, you will need the appropriate syllabuses for all the work that is to be covered.) The syllabus will have done most of the work for you, because it will have divided the whole subject into discrete sections. This should be where you start. Some of these sections may already be of a suitable 'nibble' size. If so, fine. If not, then subdivide any very large sections into something more manageable.

Wait a minute. I'd like to know what you mean by 'more manageable'.

Remember, the object of the exercise is to split up the work into smaller sections (rather like the 'courses' of the meal), each one of which is more or less complete in itself, but not so large that it is mentally 'indigestible'. So, if some topics in the syllabus occupy only a page or two of your notes, several of them can be combined to give a convenient package. Other topics may occupy a large part of your notes, perhaps a quarter or a third. If this is the case, then divide these into smaller fractions so that they are less daunting when it comes to revision.

Another thing needs a mention here. Some topics are more 'digestible' than others. If you find that some reasonably sized portion is particularly difficult, then tackle a smaller part of it. Whatever you do, don't spend an excessive amount of time on a topic which gives you too much trouble. That will simply make you mentally tired.

▼

That is all very well, but I will still have all the work facing me on the table, so where is the advantage in that?

The advantage is that you *don't* have all the work facing you on the table. As I said at the outset, you are using a bad technique to start your revision. Your problem is a psychological one, so it needs a psychological solution.

You have assumed that, to start your revision, you need to sit down for a solid session of wading through a large mass of work. Nothing could be further from the truth. Dividing the work into discrete packages has two advantages. Firstly, the effort made in sectionalising the mass of work has already focused your mind on the material to be studied. Your subconscious will already have started to select the material with which you are reasonably happy, and also to focus your attention on the material which is likely to require more work. This really constitutes a 'mini-revision' in its own right.

Everything all right so far?

▼

Yes, but you said that there were two advantages. What is the other one?

This is the whole crux of the matter. If you think about it, you will find that there are many occasions when you, like everybody else, squanders time. There is nothing wrong with this, but when exams are approaching and time is particularly valuable, 'wasted' time can, perhaps, be put to better use. One of the things I am thinking about is the time when you are travelling (to school, college, work or whatever). If you go on the bus or train, then why not use such time rather than waste it? Instead of watching your fellow travellers or reading the paper you could be reading one of those 'digestible' sections of your work. You will have already separated these into easily assimilated packages, so that five or ten minutes spent in reading through one section of your notes will bring the material to the forefront of your mind and highlight any problems which you may have.

The advantage is that you will not have used any 'valuable' time, but simply time which would otherwise have been wasted. Time normally spent in tea breaks can be utilised in the same way. After all, when you have a large amount of work to do, and especially when it has to be done in a comparatively short time, little luxuries like tea breaks can be sacrificed on the altar of necessity. You will also be able to think of other times in your daily routine when you can fit in a few minutes of quick, profitable revision. In less than a week you will find you have covered all your notes for the year, and you won't have had to go through the trauma which you described initially.

▼

Are you telling me that I can do all my revision in a few spare minutes every day? I can't believe that.

No. I didn't say that. What I am saying is that, rather than subject yourself to the problem of facing a full year's work, with all its associated problems, you can use some of your 'spare' time to do a quick survey of the course work. This corresponds to an *initial* foray into your revision. OK?

▼

Yes. All that seems fine, but I am not taking one exam, I'm taking several. I'll never get through all the work if it's going to take me a week just skimming over every topic which I need to revise.

Believe it or not, you can even turn that situation to your advantage. A common problem with revision is that it is very easy to become stale by concentrating too much on a single topic. By 'nibbling' at several different topics in succession, you can still cover the work, but avoid becoming bogged down with a single subject. Don't misunderstand me, though. I am not advocating flitting from subject to subject as a principle; what I mean is that, during your initial revision, if you come to the end of one topic area, and the next one is a large one which may take more time than you can spare at that precise moment – or, if you have had enough of that particular subject – then switch to a different subject altogether. The work needs to be done anyway, so this approach will still constitute progress.

▼

Let me recap here. You are recommending me to use the syllabus to indicate the areas of each subject which can be revised superficially as a separate package in its own right. Large topics can be broken down and small ones built up. Each of these can then be looked at, quickly, in periods which would otherwise be wasted. I can either do this with each subject in isolation, or I can switch from one subject to another, depending upon the size of the section involved, and how easy or difficult I'm finding it.

Now, unless I'm very careful, I could lose track of my progress in each subject, so I suppose that you recom-

mend that I use bits of paper, or something like that, to indicate which parts of each topic I've looked at?

Yes. Excellent. You are getting to grips with the *technique* of controlling your revision and, hopefully, finding the whole job less daunting. However, before we leave this topic, there is one other point which needs to be made. When I said divide your subject material into different portions, I did not mean that you need to do this literally. You *could* do, and there is a psychological advantage in facing a small sheaf of notes rather than a large mass representing a full year's work. The disadvantage of this system is that your notes can more easily get muddled or even lost if you separate the various parts of each subject. It all depends on your system of keeping notes, but generally speaking, it would be as well to place markers in your notes to indicate the progress of your revision. There are no hard and fast rules about this, just pick whatever method suits you best.

▼

So far, everything you have said makes sense, but I've got a couple more questions I'd like you to answer. Firstly, what about people who are taking a lot of exams? For example, some people doing GCSEs may take eight or even more exams. They can't get through all that work in little periods like tea breaks. And another thing, sometimes it simply isn't possible to revise during tea breaks. People make so much noise, and there may be nowhere to go to get any peace and quiet. Then what about people who don't go to work (or school or whatever) on the bus or train? They don't have the sort of revision time that you are talking about. Your system won't work for those people, will it?

You are quite correct on both points, but I think that you may have misunderstood a part of what I was trying to say. Let me take your second objection first.

Examination candidates who don't have travelling

time or tea breaks in which to revise will simply need to use time at home to do the necessary work. In the evenings, for example. What I am saying is, *if* you have odd bits of free time that could productively be spent on revision, then take advantage of them.

That also answers your first query. If you have a lot of exams to prepare for, then some time will have to be spent at home in doing the initial, superficial revision. Let me stress this once again, don't go into too much depth with your study at this stage. All this is happening some weeks before the exams (see box on page 101), *before* you start your serious programme of revision. Just skim over the surface to get a general idea of the work to be covered. What you need is a sort of overall 'index' of all the examinable material.

▼

Right then, if I have more than a couple of exams, I'll do the review of all the rest of them during one evening and that will cut down the amount of time needed to complete the initial survey.

That depends on what you mean. If you intend to cover, say, six subjects in one session, with the idea of getting all of the preliminary work out of the way quickly, then I would say definitely *no*.

▼

I don't see why. After all, if I study for two hours, I'll make twice the progress that I'd make in one hour, and if I put in four hours' work, I'll make four times the progress. That's only common sense isn't it?

It is certainly a belief shared by an uncommonly large number of people. But in fact, with respect, it should be called common *nonsense*!

Let me explain. It's all to do with the way in which the brain works.

▼

Wait a minute. You may be interested in how the brain works, but I've got to prepare for exams. I can't afford the time to be bothered about things like that. Later, maybe, but not now. Once I've got over the initial problem of facing a pile of revision, I can save time by squeezing a lot of work into one concentrated session. OK?

Actually, your argument isn't sound, but, if you prefer, we'll forget the brain for the moment and look at your physical well-being instead.

With all this studying, you may well get out of condition. Perhaps you feel that a bit of jogging may help to keep you fit? All right, consider half an hour of jogging. Fine. Why not do an hour and get twice as much benefit? If it comes to that, why not jog for two hours and get four times as much benefit?

Have I made my point yet? Unless you are in training for a marathon, your last, fourth, half hour of jogging is not going to do you anything like as much good as the first half hour. In all probability, just the reverse. In fact, you may finish up so tired as to be useless for anything for the rest of the day. If you must do two hours, then you will get much more benefit by having four *well separated* half-hour sessions rather than a single concentrated one.

Your brain works pretty much the same way. You can exhaust it if you try to concentrate too much work into a single session. (Perhaps we should call it the 'Banquet Syndrome'.) Have I made my point yet?

▼

All right. Yes. I accept that I can dull my senses by doing too much work in one session, so I'll break up the initial survey of work into small, easily digested packages.

Have you any more advice before we proceed to the more serious and detailed aspects of revision?

Yes. During your initial survey, you will identify the parts of the material with which you are reasonably happy. Equally, you will come across parts of your notes which appear more complex. Perhaps you had difficulty in understanding these topics when they were dealt with originally. Mark these. Use a pencil to make appropriate comments in the margins to draw your attention to possible problem areas when it comes to the more detailed revision at the next stage. These pencilled marks can be erased later, when any problems have been resolved.

Are there any more questions before we come to the more detailed aspects of revision?

▼

No. Not really. I can't foresee any major difficulties with the initial work. I suppose that the next step is to go through all the material in more detail.

Yes. It may well be that one revision session is enough to bring your mind up to date with some aspects of the syllabus and if this is the case, then so much the better – although the need for some self-assessment cannot be overlooked. (We'll be considering that in Chapter 9.) Alternatively, it may well be that some areas require much more work, especially if you haven't kept up to date on a weekly basis. If this is the case, it is possible that a whole topic could present you with difficulties. Your choice is whether to deal with that topic or skip over it and get on with another, easier one. The likelihood is that you will find yourself skipping a lot of topics, so, instead, I would recommend you to study the first problem topic as soon as you come to it. In other words, read through your notes until you discover where the first difficulty lies and then tackle it.

▼

That seems sensible enough to me. Now, let us suppose that I come to a topic with which I am utterly baffled. Suppose it's a big topic and it's going to take a long time to cover it all thoroughly. Since you've already made me

---

'Cramming' is not the answer

Many students make the mistake of thinking that revision consists of concentrating on a considerable amount of work shortly before the examinations are due. This technique is a poor one and should be avoided. Revision is best done *throughout the course of study*.

Shortly after a class or lecture, the subject matter is fresh in your mind and this is the best time to consolidate your understanding of it. Small points which appear obvious at this time, but which are not covered fully in your notes, may well make much less sense after a few weeks. You may even forget them altogether with the passage of time.

If, at this stage, there is anything in the material that you don't understand, tackle the problem as soon as possible. If you can't sort it out for yourself, find some other source of information. Try other text books and, if that fails, ask the teacher or lecturer. Leaving such problems unresolved until just before the exams is a mistake. You may not have enough time then!

---

a bit cautious about doing too much work in one session, how much work do I put into that problem topic?

The answer to that lies partly in yourself and partly in the pattern of the way in which your brain works. I know that you want to avoid this, but a little information about it will convince you of its worth, believe me.

In any period of study, the amount of material which your brain retains depends upon the length of time for which you study. The *first* fraction of time spent is usually the most efficient. By that I mean that the material in the first fraction of time is retained best. After all, the first period of study is when your brain is at its freshest, so it tends to understand and retain material better. The material revised during the *last* fraction of time is also retained fairly well. Other things being equal, the last thing you read is, naturally, likely to be retained. But this does rely on your mind being reasonably fresh. If it is saturated with the work done previously, then it is possible that it will retain nothing – but let us assume that you are being sensible and you are not going to let that happen.

The middle bit is the problem section. This part is the least efficient of all. Unless there is something of particular interest, then this section will be less efficiently retained by the brain.

▼

I can accept what you are saying. Two one-hour periods of revision are better than a single two-hour period, and, perhaps, four half-hour periods are better still. But you still haven't answered my question. How long should each study period last? You seem to be reluctant to answer that one.

Your question is like asking me 'How long is a piece of string?' The answer varies according to a number of factors, but the string concept can be used to advantage. In fact, instead of string, let us take a clothes line as an example. The starting part, at the first support, is held high and acts efficiently for drying wet clothes. The same applies to the end part, at the other support. The middle bit is the part that sags. The amount by which it sags depends upon the length of the line (which represents the length of time of study). The longer the line, the more it sags. There is an advantage, therefore, in keeping the length of line (and the period of study) short.

Another thing which affects the amount of sag is the weight of the washing on the line. Some of the academic material which you study may be 'heavy going', corresponding to a heavy article on the line. In this case the line needs to be shorter than for the lighter stuff – hence study periods should be correspondingly shorter. (All of this assumes that your mind is in a reasonably active state, i.e. that you are not mentally tired.)

Now, perhaps, you can understand why it is difficult to be precise about the duration of each period of study. As a general rule, though, for subjects which you find easy, an hour should be about the limit. In some cases three-quarters of an hour might be better. With difficult material, something in the order of ten to fifteen minutes may be more appropriate. It is largely up to you. Whatever the case may be, when you start to feel that the studying is getting too difficult then, depending on your state of mind, move on to something else or stop altogether.

▼

Wait a minute, you have just contradicted yourself. When you used jogging as an example, you said that the last *half hour wouldn't do much good, possibly even more harm than good. Now you're saying that the last period of study is retained better than the middle bit. Make your mind up.*

Sorry, but you've misunderstood me. The last half hour of jogging was after a *preceding* ninety minutes, so that during that last half hour you would be pretty tired (unless you were extremely fit). When studying, you would still be comparatively fresh during the last five minutes of a forty-five minute period. The last five minutes of a two-, three- or four-hour period of studying is likely to be a different thing altogether. Is it all clear now?

▼

Yes. Problem solved.

The next problem is, when it comes to the more serious revision, how much of my notes should I revise? Some of my colleagues seem to think that it isn't possible to do everything, so they are choosing only a part of each subject for revision and then hope for the best.

Beware of saturation

During revision, and especially when you feel you are making considerable progress, it is possible to be carried away with your enthusiasm.

It is easy (and you may have already experienced this) to read a page of notes, or a page of a book, and reach the bottom without realising what you have read. If this ever happens, *stop*. You will do no good by trying to cram information into a saturated or bored mind. Your mind *must* be receptive if any benefit is to be obtained and this is one of the reasons for the 'nibbling' technique.

It may well be that you have set yourself a target of work to complete, but if you reach the state described above, your time would be better employed in taking a rest, ending that period of revision altogether or replacing it with a period of self-assessment (see Chapter 9).

A word of warning is needed here. Saturation will prevent any efficient revision, but this will only happen *after* a session of study. You will be fooling only yourself if you use it as an excuse for not starting a period of revision.

That is a very questionable choice of tactics and again, it is not possible to give a neat little answer to apply to every situation. Once again, it depends on you. I'm not being deliberately evasive – the circumstances will dictate the line of action which is the best one to take.

Let us take the simplest possibility first, an internal examination, set by your teacher or lecturer, at the end of an intermediate year of study. In this case, you will be preparing for an examination covering a single year's work, so the amount of material will be limited. The topics on the examination paper are likely to cover *all* the material dealt with during the year, so it would be prudent to do likewise with your examination revision.

Once again, the form of the exam could dictate your revision plan to a large extent. With the multiple-choice type of exam, you may be required to answer *all* the questions set, and these are likely to cover the entire syllabus for the year. Your revision should, therefore, cover everything. Alternatively, when the exam consists of essay-type answers and there is a choice of questions, it may be possible to omit certain parts of the syllabus during revision. Remember, though, that this technique actually *reduces your choice* of questions during the exam itself, so that any initial advantage of choice that you may have had will be cancelled out (partly or totally) by your incomplete preparation. If you have to answer, say, five questions out of eight, and you only revise five major topics, what do you do if you are faced with a question you haven't foreseen, covering an aspect of the topic you haven't considered in depth? This can happen. Under circumstances such as these, I would again advise you to revise everything.

At the other extreme, we have exams which we might refer to as 'Finals', i.e. exams taken at the end of a course of study lasting some years, which involve questions which could be taken from any part of the overall syllabus. In this case, the situation is, obviously, different. There will be a vast amount of work to be covered and it is often unlikely that *everything* can be revised with the sort of thoroughness that might be given to the less taxing exams. In such a case, a certain amount of selection is needed.

▼

Yes, I know. Some people try to predict the likelihood of certain questions cropping up by analysing past exam papers. Don't you think that that is a good idea?

Not really. Whatever you call it, it amounts to gambling

with your exams and that can rarely be regarded as a sensible technique. After all, the outcome may be that you fail to obtain your qualification, your diploma or degree or whatever. Whilst it is true that you may be able to retake the exams at a later date, you will still be gambling with your final qualification. No, it is better to be rather more systematic about revision.

Incidentally, the same applies to assuming that an exam paper is going to have an identical structure to those of previous years. Often it does, but you cannot claim 'Unfair!' if a new external examiner decides to bring a fresh look to an exam structure which has been in operation for a long time.

▼

So, if trying to predict questions is not a good idea, and if it isn't possible to revise everything as fully as I need, what should I do?

First of all, you must realise that it is absolutely essential for you to answer the required number of questions, no more and certainly no less. I won't go into the reasons for this here because it is covered in Chapter 11. At this point, just take my word for it.

The second step is to refer back to the results of your initial survey of the syllabus for the exam. You will have identified the topics at which you feel that you could excel and, in some ways more importantly, the topics which will give you trouble. It is a good idea to list all the topics which could appear on the exam paper and make your own personal comments alongside each topic. Your comments should fall into three categories: the topics which you find easy, those which are not so bad and those which you find particularly difficult. We will assume that a reasonable amount of work will deal with the first two. It is the third group which needs your attention.

Identify the topics which are going to present you with difficulties and note how many there are. Then determine what fraction of the whole the difficult topics correspond to. Do this in the context of the number of topics that could be on the exam paper. If the number of difficult topic areas is low, say two or three out of a total of fifteen or so, then it won't do too much harm to omit those from your revision. In other words, if you feel that, *with adequate revision*, you will be able to make a good job of answering questions corresponding to twelve topic areas out of a possible total of fifteen, then concentrate on those twelve and omit the other three. As a broad rule, you should be prepared to do a good job of answering about *twice as many* questions as you would be expected to be asked on the paper.

However, a real problem crops up if the number of 'difficult' topics corresponds to a large fraction of the total. It would be most unwise to gamble on the major part of the exam paper containing the topics which you find easy.

▼

Let me see if I've got this right. What you're saying is that, if I feel happy with most of the topics which could appear on the paper, then, with proper revision, I shouldn't have too much to worry about. On the other hand, if I find that a large fraction of the work is likely to present me with problems, then I need to – well, do what?

This problem resolves itself into fairly simple terms. The issue is not how much must you prepare for, but rather, how much can you manage to *omit* and still have the best overall chance of success in the exam.

What it boils down to is this. Your preparation for the exam must ensure that the *minimum* amount of material is excluded from your revision. Your line of attack now comes down to identifying the topics which you would find *extremely difficult* to attempt. Valuable revision time could be wasted on these topics, so it would be better and more profitably spent on those other, rather easier topics. You must be honest about this though. It is very easy to dislike a topic and place it in the 'extremely difficult' category when, in fact, more work on your part could

Are your notes complete?

Many candidates assume that their lecture notes cover all the material that could appear on the exam paper. This attitude is not always sound, particularly at the higher academic levels such as degree courses. Obviously if you have been absent through sickness or any other reason you will have missed out on work, and it is all too easy to forget to catch up on this. You may also be expected to supplement what is covered in class with reading or research of your own.

The lesson is simple. Ensure that you are prepared to answer the material which is *on the syllabus*, not just that which is in your notes. They may not be identical.

By the way, by 'notes' I mean anything that provides you with information about your course of study – not only your own notes, but any hand-outs you may have had from the tutor or teacher, and possibly additional material in text books or periodicals that you have been advised to read.

make the subject considerably more approachable (re-read what I said in Chapter 3 about pet hates and see if you can find a fresh viewpoint). This is another reason why I claim that consistent revision throughout the academic year is the best policy. It can save an awful lot of distress later, when exams are looming on the horizon.

One more point. Although what I have just said referred to 'Finals', in principle, the same considerations apply to *any* exam. In other words, it would be wise to prepare yourself to give good answers to at least *twice as many* topics as you would expect to find on the exam paper.

▼

What you have said is all very well if the number of difficult topics is small, but what happens if the difficult topics prove to be a large fraction of the total? It means that I have a hard slog ahead of me, doesn't it?

It might seem like that initially, but it need not be as bad as you may think. Obviously, a lot of work will need to be done, but that doesn't mean that you will have to spend hours and hours on subjects which you find uninteresting. Once again, and I can't emphasise this enough, it's all a matter of technique.

Many students, when they encounter a difficult or uninteresting topic, tend to avoid it. But avoiding a difficult topic simply puts the problem off until another day. Furthermore, the longer you put the problem off, the more reluctant you will be to tackle it later. The earlier you face it, the quicker you will master it.

Here is a method that works for a lot of people. Identify a problem topic and select a small portion of it. At your next session of revision, tackle this topic first. See how you manage with ten minutes. Can you manage fifteen minutes – or even twenty – before things start to get difficult? Whatever the length of time is, *stop* as soon as the going gets tough (as long as this is not in the first few seconds). After this, give yourself a little 'reward'. Do half an hour of revision on a topic which you find easy. After this, your mind will be more settled and you will feel that you have achieved something worthwhile. Then go back to the difficult topic. Do you need to retrace your initial steps to reinforce what you did earlier, or can you make more progress? Do whatever is necessary, but only *you* can decide what that is.

Naturally, this technique can be used with each of the more difficult topics so that, in a comparatively short period of time you will become more at ease with revising difficult and more straightforward material within the same revision session. There is also another advantage. The topics which you originally thought to be particularly difficult, may, with this sort of treatment, appear to be not quite so bad after all.

▼

Wait a minute. Something doesn't sound right. So far you have been telling me to spend less time on the difficult topics than on the easy ones. Surely you don't really mean that.

What we have been dealing with so far has been the *earlier* stage of revision: identifying the problem topics, then the initial approach to the problem. The next stage is to get closer to the problems and overcome them. We are back to the analogy of climbing a flight of stairs. You can revise easy topics two stairs at a time, so to speak. The difficult ones need to be taken more slowly, and you will need to spend more time in order to reach the required level of understanding of the subject. You will eventually spend more time on the difficult material, in the form of shorter sessions, but more of them. What most people find, though, is that the more practice they get with difficult material, the less difficult it becomes. The old saying 'practice makes perfect' applies just as much to revision as it does to anything else.

Is it all clearer now?

▼

Yes. I'm happier about tackling those 'difficult' topics, but there is one thing you haven't even touched upon. So far you have mentioned using 'spare' time to do the original, superficial revision. That's OK, but what about the best time for doing the serious revision? I've heard of people being divided into two categories, the 'early birds' who work best in the mornings and the 'night owls' who perform their best at night. Should revision be reserved for one or other of these two times?

What you say about early morning and late night workers

is quite true, but it doesn't mean that people *can't* work satisfactorily at other times – otherwise shift work would not be possible.

Really, it's all a matter of practicalities. If you are better in the mornings *and* you are able to revise at that time, so much the better. The revision you do then is likely to be more efficient than what you do at the end of the day when you are tired.

On the other hand, most people have constraints on their time which mean their revision is restricted to evenings. This is far from ideal, not only for 'early birds', because evenings are the normal social or leisure time for most people. However, if you are at work or school or college during the day, you have no real option. The good news is that if you have started your revision early enough, you shouldn't have to give up every hour of every evening to studying.

▼

That's a point I wanted to bring up. So far you haven't mentioned anything to do with when I should revise. By that I don't mean what time of day, I mean how long before the exams should I start?

Good question. I gave a rough timetable for revision on page 101, but let's look at this important subject in more detail.

As we have seen, the best possible technique for revision and to avoid the trauma of end-of-session 'cramming' is to make sure that you understand the subject material *as early as possible*. Look at it this way. If you set aside some time *every week* for the purpose of revising the week's work and making sure you understand it, you might be able to cover it in a couple of hours. Think of the effort you would have to put in if, instead, you had to do thirty or more times as much work nearer the end of the session, i.e. just before the exams, to cover a full year's work. Multiply that by the number of subjects in which you are going to be examined and you'll realise that you are giving yourself a considerable amount of trouble. Moreover, it's *avoidable* trouble.

▼

That sounds all very well, but I can't see any point in learning all that stuff early, if I'm going to forget it, months later, just before the exams. I'll just have to do the same work all over again.

That is not quite true. We considered this in Chapter 7, when we were discussing memory. To recap, once you have *understood* a subject properly, it takes very little effort to bring it to the forefront of your mind later – considerably less effort than trying to understand it in a concentrated 'cramming' period immediately before the exams. The real point is that once you have learned something, you don't have to *relearn* it, you simply have to refresh your memory. And this takes very little effort, compared to the initial understanding process.

To make things even easier, you should set aside a *regular* period or periods during the week when your revision takes place. Arrange it to suit yourself. It doesn't have to clash with your favourite TV programme or any special social activity, as long as you stick to your revision timetable *rigidly*. (Very few people manage to catch up on a lost period of study by having a 'double period' at a later date.) The advantage in organising your revision in this way is that it becomes such a part of your life (during the academic year) that, once your system has been established, you will think nothing of it. It won't be a chore, you won't resent it, it will simply be a part of your study system.

▼

You're not saying that I have to go through everything every week? Surely you mean just my lecture notes for that particular week.

Of course. There is no point in going over material which you have revised the week before, *but* I didn't simply mean lecture notes. There are plenty of other sources of information to which you may need to refer. For example, 'hand-outs'. When you receive these, do you actually read them, or just file them away to be looked at some time in the future? In my experience, less than five per cent of students I dealt with bothered to refer to hand-outs straight away. More often, they were reserved for the last-minute cramming sessions.

Another source of information is returned course exercises and 'test' exam papers. Don't neglect these as a part of your ongoing revision. Learn from your own mistakes and the tutor's comments. Go over these immediately when your teacher or lecturer will be available to clear up any misunderstandings. This may not apply later, and you may even forget to pursue these topics if you omit them for too long.

One thing that many students do not realise until too late is that there is a considerable *dis*advantage in *not* revising in this manner, and you may have already experienced this. At the last minute, the library books to which you desperately want to refer are often unavailable. The other 'crammers' are using them!

▼

So, if I work throughout the year, keeping up to date with all the new material, I shouldn't need to do too much revision just before the exam. Right?

Partly right. It all depends upon how well you retain the work you have revised and, of course, how easy or difficult you find the subject. I would suggest that your revision technique involves the following steps. As I said before, on a weekly basis, keep up to date with all the course material. Secondly, start your serious revision about six to eight weeks before the examination time (or earlier, if you feel that it is necessary). Go through all the course work necessary for the exam and make your assessment of the 'easy' and 'difficult' material. This is the initial, casual survey which I mentioned earlier. The 'difficult' topics will need more of your attention, so concentrate on those in 'nibble-sized' portions. By the time the exams are about a week away, most of the hard work should have been done, but any isolated areas needing study can receive special attention.

The night before each exam is *not* the time to do any further new studying. If you haven't revised some topic or other, omit it. Spend the evening relaxing or doing some fairly easy revision for a different subject. But whatever you do, *don't* spend it on a concentrated session of revision, especially not on the subject of tomorrow's exam. Also, make sure that you get to bed reasonably early.

Finally, don't worry about the exam. You will have done everything possible by this time – worrying can do no good whatsoever, but it can do a lot of harm (refer to Chapter 6 if help is needed here).

Oh, there is one other point regarding the time immediately before the exams. Make sure that you get to the examination room *early*. It will do your state of mind no good at all if you have to rush because you hadn't started out in good time.

▶ Summary ◀

1. Don't depress yourself by looking at a whole year's (or course's) work as a single entity for revision.
2. Use the syllabus to help you make natural divisions between subject areas.
3. Split the material to be studied into small packages which can be studied over short periods of time.
4. Use any 'spare' time (e.g. when travelling or during tea breaks) to do your initial, superficial revision.
5. If you can't use travelling time or tea breaks (and/or if you have several exams to prepare for), you should still divide time spent studying at home into easily managed portions.
6. Switch revision between subjects in order to avoid becoming bored with any single topic. Don't avoid

'difficult' subjects. Tackle one of these first, then ease the load with an 'easy' one.

7. Even if you have a few hours for revision, do not attempt to cover too much work in any single session. Give yourself frequent short breaks (of self-assessment, if appropriate).

8. Don't gamble by trying to predict exam questions in order to select topics for revision.

9. If, for whatever reason, it is not possible to revise *all* of the subject material, then select the very *minimum* of topics to avoid revising. Attempt to revise enough material to answer *twice as many* questions as the examiner will require you to answer.

10. Periods of revision of 'difficult' subjects may be shorter than for 'easy' ones, but you will require more of them.

11. Don't restrict your revision to class notes. Use *all* available sources of information (e.g. marked course work, returned test papers, 'hand-outs' and text books).

12. 'Cramming' just before exams is the worst technique for revision. Not only is it very inefficient, it also produces considerable stress. Constant, steady work, done on a regular basis throughout the course, is virtually guaranteed to give a much greater likelihood of success.

Chapter 9

▼

Self-assessment

*Don't let the examiner judge you on your revision
— do that for yourself.*
Brian Duncalf

*There is nothing so obscure as our own ignorance,
for it is only when we begin to destroy it that we
discover that it ever existed.*
Brian Duncalf

Many sources of advice for examination candidates mix the subjects of revision and self-assessment and place them under the general heading of 'revision'. In fact, they are two different subjects, and they need to be treated as such.

In many respects, revision and self-assessment are similar to memory and recall, which was considered in Chapter 7, in as much as revision is the absorption of information (or 'data storage') and self-assessment is equivalent to recollection of information (or 'data retrieval'). The difference with self-assessment is that it includes, or should include, evaluation of the *quality* of the recalled information and its value in the context of the examination(s) being taken. In other words, there is little point in being able to recall information which has been revised if the information is incomplete. Similarly, even if the recalled information is complete, it will be of little value if it cannot be *used* satisfactorily on the examination script. To take an analogy, think what would happen if you didn't plan a route for a holiday properly. It is

Exams and Intelligence

There are far too many students who claim, 'I'm not very bright, so I won't do well at exams.' These people put themselves at a disadvantage for no good reason. Here's why.

Examinations, like quizzes, are not about being highly intelligent, they are about being *well informed*. Even the most intelligent people can fail examinations if they are poorly informed, but if you are well informed and you can express yourself adequately, then you can pass *any* examination – *irrespective of your level of intelligence*.

There isn't a great deal you can do to improve your intelligence, but the preparation for your exams is in *your* hands and nobody else's!

pointless to make a detailed plan of the beginning and of the end of the route if the middle part is omitted. Similarly, a complete route will be far from satisfactory if the names of the intermediate towns or landmarks are not included or, perhaps, if the road numbers are omitted. The same considerations apply here.

Imagine that you are going to perform on stage, playing a musical instrument, say, or performing in a play or pantomime. How do you prepare for that performance? What you *don't* do is read the music or script and leave it at that. You *practise* or *rehearse*, alone or with the other performers. You continue to do this until your performance is as near perfection as you can manage. Doesn't the preparation for your exams deserve as much effort? After all, if you make a mess of your stage performance, you will only suffer a little embarrassment and even that will be forgotten (or at least become insignificant) in a short time. With examinations, your successes will be with you for the rest of your life.

Self-assessment is the rehearsal for examinations, and it can be practised in a number of different ways, alone or with others. The best method involves writing, but this is not essential. The advantage is that you can use whichever method suits you best, and there are plenty of methods from which you can choose.

▶ Mixing Revision and Self-Assessment ◀

I mentioned in the previous chapter that sessions of intensive revision can lead to mental saturation. The problem is that once you have overcome any initial resistance to revision and, so to speak, have 'got into gear', the revision tends to become easier and your involvement with it easier still. It is then quite easy to spend a couple of hours, or even more, in concentrated reading, almost without realising it. This can produce the impression of great progress but, in fact, that impression can be an illusion.

As we have seen, there is a limit to the amount of information which the brain can absorb in any single session, so the practice of reading lecture notes or text books for hours on end is a very inefficient one. The difficulty is that different people have different capacities for study, so it is not possible to give precise figures for the length of time for which any individual should attempt to take in information. This is where self-assessment comes into play, as the incorporation of other useful work into revision gives a double bonus. The first is that it helps to avoid excessive reading and the associated potential for mental saturation. Secondly, it provides a means of checking the value of the material you have been studying. It should go without saying that it is pointless to continue to read further if you are not absorbing and understanding the essence of the material you have read previously.

Before going into the details of methods of self-

Continuity

No subject is composed simply of a jumbled mixture of isolated facts. There is always a continuous flow from one item to the next and your programme of self-assessment should include testing this continuity.

Try this little exercise. Select a street or road in your town which you pass along very frequently. Choose one with a series of neighbouring shops, say about twenty in all. Now suppose a stranger asks for directions to a particular shop somewhere in the middle of the row. Starting from one end, could you tell him how many *doors* along the series the shop can be found? Keep in mind that some doors may not be entrances to businesses, but may give access to private premises.

Unless you are a customer (or window shopper) of *every* shop, it is unlikely that you will be able to answer this accurately. Few people could, because an item of information which is of no immediate interest (in this case, one or more of the shops) is not stored subconsciously in the memory.

The same principles apply to your revision and self-assessment. If you don't make a special effort to deal with *every* point in a series within a topic, then you are likely to have gaps in your understanding which could contribute to a poor performance answering some related question.

assessment, it may be of value to revise its purpose. The object of an examination is to convince the examiner that you are aware of, and understand, certain aspects of some specified subject. In order to do this, you should be able to convince *yourself* that you understand that subject. Therefore, you must act as your own examiner. If you can convince yourself that you are adequately familiar with some topic, then you can progress; if not, you need to go back over the material until you *are* satisfied.

▶ Don't take the easy way out ◀

During the processes of revision and self-assessment, it is very tempting to select 'easy' topics. This will certainly help to boost your confidence but it also incurs a measure of self-deception. Examiners do not normally go out of their way to choose 'easy' topics for examinations. Nor should you.

Most subjects are progressive to some extent – that is, each stage of a course builds on knowledge gained earlier in your studies – so it follows that the study of those subjects should follow a parallel path. In other words, tackle each subject as it was dealt with during the term, 'difficult' topics included. If the subject contains a number of individual, progressive topic areas, then this technique will ensure that 'easy' and 'difficult' aspects of each subject will alternate during revision and self-assessment and thereby provide the variety which will minimise the risk of boredom or mental saturation. Mathematics provides a typical example. Arithmetic, algebra and geometry are often studied in parallel in the same year and the subject material in each becomes increasingly 'difficult' with progressive study. So if you work on arithmetic first, then progress to algebra, say, you can alternate the 'easy' bits of algebra with the difficult bits of arithmetic. Similarly, by the time you have reached the difficult stages of algebra, you can be starting on the easy bits of geometry.

▶ Finding the Questions ◀

One of the greatest difficulties examination candidates experience is knowing what questions to ask themselves. Obviously, you know about what you know. The real question is, how do you discover what you do *not* know?

Ready-Made Topics for Self-Assessment

Questions set during the course (and your answers) can provide an ideal sample of the sort of thing which is suitable for self-assessment. The same applies to examination questions from previous years' papers. After revision, use those questions to test yourself. Avoid referring to your notes during this process. Don't prompt yourself in this way but, rather, use your apparent need to do so as an indication of the weaknesses in your knowledge. Use these references only as a last resort, as it is important for you to *think deeply* about gaps in your understanding. If you can work out your problems without reference to your notes under these conditions, then you will certainly be able to do it under examination conditions!

The identification of whole blocks of ignorance is not the issue. These should be self-evident and they can be isolated for further concentrated study. What is more obscure is the *gap*, or gaps, in each topic area. How can you discover where these lie? They can't be highlighted for further study because you don't know whether they exist or not. So, if they do, how do you identify *what* they are?

The process of self-assessment is intended to answer such questions.

▶ Selecting the Topics ◀

Chapter 8 included methods of dividing a year's work into easily managed portions for the purpose of revision and these same fractions of a syllabus can be used as a starting point for self-assessment. It is important that, after revision, the topic to be self-tested should form a complete package of information in its own right. The reason for this is that, in order to evaluate the revision, you must assess each package of information *from beginning to end*; otherwise, the continuity of the subject may be lost. In other words, if an otherwise complete subject is split into say two sections, then you may appear to understand both of them satisfactorily, but the *link* between the two may be lost. This would correspond to one of the 'gaps' mentioned earlier.

▶ Talking It Through ◀

This is the simplest method of self-assessment and one that can be employed not only during serious study periods, but also at virtually any time when there are no significant distractions. It involves selecting a complete topic and explaining all about it *to yourself*. Do this as though you were a teacher in front of a class. Don't miss anything out. Assume that your class has never heard *anything at all* about the subject, no matter how simple or self-evident it may appear to be. Don't be afraid to interrupt yourself with a question from 'the class' – the more searching the question, the more value you will obtain from the exercise.

You can practise this process on the bus or train, or anywhere where you will not be disturbed. When I was studying for a degree, I worked during the day and went to evening classes four nights a week. I did my revision and self-assessment after the evening classes. It was the worst possible way to study, but there were no alternatives at that time. After a period of revision, I used to take my dog for a long walk in the early hours of the morning and used the technique described above to instruct him (aloud) about the subject I had been revising. He didn't learn much, but the process did *me* a great deal of good. In some respects I was lucky, because we were the only ones around at that time in the morning: I wouldn't recommend following this advice quite so literally within earshot of other people!

▶ **Recording Your Thoughts** ◀

One drawback to the previous technique of self-assessment is that you will have no record of what you have said. Hence, it is possible to overlook some aspect of a topic which you have 'explained' to yourself. One remedy is to tape your answers. A tape-recorder will not only assist in getting your material down on record but, as you listen to the playback, you can simultaneously refer to your notes to check the accuracy and completeness of your answers.

A further advantage of this method is that you will have a record of your thoughts and, if the process of reading your notes presents any problems, an audible record may be more help. You can also use tapes instead of notes for revision if you find this useful. Using headphones instead of spectacles is also a good way of avoiding eye strain!

▶ **Using an Assistant** ◀

Another method of assessing the value of your revision is to ask someone else to listen to what you have to say. Willing help of this kind may be difficult to find, or it may be available only on spasmodic occasions. Nevertheless, it can be of considerable value.

You can ask your helper simply to listen to you and to determine whether your explanation of the topic can be easily understood. In this instance you should ensure that your helper is *not* too familiar with the subject material, otherwise it is always possible for him/her to fill in the parts which you omit. If you can give a convincing and understandable explanation to a person who is totally ignorant of the topic, then you should certainly be able to convince the examiner of your mastery of the material in question.

Another way in which an assistant can be of use is for

him/her to refer to your notes and ask you questions about them. Definitions and similar factual points are particularly suitable for treatment in this way. It is also less boring for the assistant, who becomes more involved in the process and less of a 'victim' as a listener.

Using an assistant can become even more helpful when he (or she) is another student on the same course, although problems can arise for reasons mentioned above. It is absolutely imperative that prompting or filling in missing gaps is avoided, for obvious reasons. However, fellow students can take turns in questioning, and, even better, 'tripping each other up' on selected topics.

There can be further benefit if disagreements crop up about facts or their interpretation. Under such circumstances, no party should simply submit to the opinions of the other on the assumption that they are better informed. Each student should attempt to convince the other that his understanding of the subject is the correct one, and be prepared to defend his position when challenged. Friendly disagreements of this type can be very effective in identifying weaknesses in understanding. When disagreements cannot be resolved logically between the individual parties, then external help will be needed. However, the dispute will have served its purpose of identifying problems, as this is what self-assessment is all about.

▶ Mock Exams ◀

One of the best methods, if not *the* best method of self-assessment consists of setting yourself questions and answering them under examination conditions. Questions can be derived by the methods described above, i.e. from work set during the course and from past examination papers, although there is no reason why you should not just make up suitable questions. If you do, it is important to set questions which are not too simple, otherwise the benefit of the exercise will be lost.

This method has several advantages, not the least of

Message received and understood?

The object of an examination is for you to communicate personally with your examiner. You do this (with a few obvious exceptions, such as multiple choice questions and practical exams) by means of your handwriting. Most of us, given time, can produce a neat, legible, written account of what we want to say but, during exams, time is one thing we don't have in abundance. It follows, therefore, that during exams you are likely to try to write quickly and lose some of that legibility. So always keep in mind the fact that all of your year's work, your preparation for the exam and your *correct answers* will come to nothing if the examiner cannot read your script!

Another point which may need stressing is that the examiner may have several dozen (or even several hundred) scripts to mark. It is not reasonable for you to expect him to spend a great deal of time trying to decipher your scribble if you can't be bothered to communicate with him properly.

Try the following test. Take your time and write out a short passage of four or five sentences. It doesn't matter what it is, but make sure that what you write does not include your name, address or anything else which will help a reader to identify you as the writer.

Next, imagine that you are under examination conditions and pressed for time. Write the same message at the speed you think you would use during an exam.

Finally, ask somebody (or, better still, several people) to read what you have written and comment on the ease with which they did so. Do this test for yourself also. Everybody involved (and that includes you!) should be as objective and honest as possible.

Take note of what is said, especially if the remarks are not very complimentary. Remember your examiner is going to be one of those people soon!

them being that it gives a good indication of the *time* needed to answer questions satisfactorily under exam conditions. The answers can also be compared with standard references (notes and text books) for accuracy and possible omissions. Not infrequently, the self-marking of these scripts offers more information than the process of revision itself.

One criticism levelled at this method of self-assessment is that it is too time-consuming, but let us consider that point. It is true that setting aside say three hours for a 'mock exam' at home is not something that many students would look forward to with enthusiasm and the benefits derived from this exercise may be less valuable than those obtained by alternating periods of self-assessment and revision. However, if the mock exam is reduced to one question at a time, requiring perhaps half an hour to answer, introducing a mock exam question into a revision period is a perfectly viable proposition.

A further advantage of this technique is that self-examined scripts together with additional comments by the 'examiner' (i.e. you) can be a particularly valuable reference in future revision; the principal point here is that the script is of *your* making, rather than somebody else's, and if you can produce material of this type for yourself, then the need to *remember* it during examinations is reduced, if not removed altogether.

▶ Index Cards ◀

Another approach to self-assessment is to use index cards. Instead of writing a full answer to a question, the response is abbreviated to an *outline* of each of the individual facts relating to the answer. In this way the main skeleton of the answer is condensed into a few fundamental remarks, each on a separate card, and you can fill in the rest of the flesh mentally, from memory.

Although this technique lacks the time-testing element of a self-set mock exam, it does retain its other advantages and offers even more. After the cards have served their purpose of self-assessment, you can record corrections and additions on them. You can then use the cards as a further source of material for revision. They will form a concentrated source of reference, highlighting the major points in the subject, but omitting the detailed material which contributes to the large volume of course notes.

▶ Summary ◀

1. Self-assessment is not the same thing as revision. It means testing the *effectiveness* of revision.
2. Self-assessment and revision should be combined to avoid excessive periods of revision and the resulting mental saturation.
3. Individual topics for self-assessment should have been identified during revision. The syllabus, course work and past examination papers all provide topics to be considered.
4. Explaining a topic to yourself is one of the easiest means of self-assessment. A tape-recorder can give a permanent record of verbal explanations.
5. An assistant may help to test the thoroughness of revision, although he/she should not prompt answers. You and a fellow student may help each other with mutual self-assessment.
6. A self-set mock examination is among the best methods of assessing the efficiency of revision.
7. Use index cards to record the main points of a subject. After correction and amendment, these can be incorporated into your revision programme.

Chapter 10

▼

Reading the Paper

*Reading is sometimes an ingenious device for
avoiding thought.*
Arthur Helps

Reading the examination paper is sometimes regarded as something of a chore, a tiresome but necessary process which robs the candidate of valuable time which should be spent in the more profitable exercise of answering the questions. The importance of reading the paper is investigated here and the value of *careful* reading of the paper emphasised.

▼

I don't think that anybody needs to tell me about how to read an exam paper. I can read – otherwise I wouldn't be taking written exams – and unless the examiner tries to cheat me by using terms I don't understand, or by asking trick questions, then that's all there is to it. All right?

No! All wrong actually. Let us put aside your so-called 'trick questions' just for the moment and concentrate on the more important matters. What most candidates don't realise is that one of the commonest causes of poor marks in exams is *not* reading the paper properly. There are plenty of pitfalls in between sitting down in the examination room and starting to write your answers. What you need is to be aware of them and avoid them. For starters, make sure that you read the rubric (or instructions) on the top of the paper.

▼

That seems a waste of time. I know what exam I'm taking and I know how much time I have, so I can save a few minutes by missing out the bit on the top of the paper.

See what I mean? That is pitfall number one. Firstly, it has been known for candidates to be given the wrong paper. It doesn't happen often, but errors like this *have* happened: Besides, the amount of reading time involved is only a matter of seconds, but it can make a lot of difference.

▼

OK, then. So the best thing to do is to read the instructions, then quickly skim through the paper until I see an easy question and get on with answering it.

That is another mistake made by an awful lot of students. Once again, it is a technique to be avoided. There are several reasons for this and they will become self-evident shortly, but for the moment let's just say that this technique will not do you justice.

Before you even think of putting pen to paper, read through all the questions carefully, and I really mean *carefully*. Whatever you do, don't rush this process.

▼

That sounds like another waste of time. When I have a limited amount of time, why should I read the whole paper when I could be answering one of the questions? After all, I can read the rest of the paper later.

The answer to this lies in the way in which your subconscious works. No matter how good your memory is, there has almost certainly been a time when you could not recall some fact. It might be the name of a person, the title of a song or something like that, but people's memories don't always deliver the results *immediately*. How many

Read the rubric!

The rubric is one example of the examiner giving you information, rather than asking you for it. It is an integral part of the examination paper and its importance should not be underestimated.

Apart from the date of the exam and the time (which you already know), the rubric tells you what the examiner wants of you. Having read previous years' papers, you may think that you know what the examination is all about. It is likely that the paper you sit will be similar in structure to the one set last year, but this is not guaranteed. Read the rubric and make sure.

One of the more important aspects of the paper is the amount of time that you have available. Make no mistake about this.

Some parts of the paper may be compulsory. Other parts may leave you with a choice, but whatever the structure of the paper is, make sure that you know *exactly* what you need to do. There should be no ambiguity about this, but if you are not sure of the requirements, ask the invigilator to clear up any possible misunderstandings at once. It is futile complaining that you didn't understand some requirement *after* the examination is over.

times, for example, have you gone to bed with a question on your mind and woken up with the answer the following morning? And this is when you are comparatively relaxed. The dusty corners of your memory banks are likely to be even more inaccessible under the stressful conditions that prevail during examinations.

How, then, do you give your memory time to locate the facts? The answer is to read the whole paper. Don't rush this, either. Take your time. In an examination lasting three hours you can take ten minutes. Even fifteen minutes is not excessive, for such time will not be wasted.

The fact is that the brain is capable of doing a lot more than we give it credit for. It can perform many tasks simultaneously and while you are reading the questions on the paper, your subconscious will be sifting through your memory and bringing the relevant facts to the surface. By the time you have read through the whole paper, the facts relating to the earlier questions will have been surveyed subconsciously. Your brain does this all the time, and it will do it now. After all, you don't have to think about telling your heart to beat or your lungs to breathe. These functions happen automatically while you are thinking about other things.

There is an added bonus to reading the whole paper. The first question which you thought was easy may, in fact, not have been the best for you to tackle. As you read on, you may find one which is more to your liking. Remember, under the circumstances that exist during examinations, there is always the risk of rushing into doing things you might regret later, so do things properly the *first time*. You may not have the time (or, for that matter, the inclination) to correct mistakes later.

▼

That's all very well, but while I'm reading the paper carefully, the others are getting on with answering the questions, so I'm going to be at a disadvantage.

Not at all. The others will still have to read the rest of the paper, but they may well have committed the blunders which you have avoided. Besides, you shouldn't bother about what the others are doing, just concentrate on doing *your* work properly.

One other thing. The time you spend in reading the paper will be taken into account when it comes to answering the questions, but this will be dealt with in more detail in the next chapter.

▼

I'm still not convinced about all that time spent on reading the paper. What can go wrong if I simply read through it quickly?

What you must remember is that reading an exam paper is not like reading a newspaper or a novel. If you misread either of these, no harm will be done and, if necessary, you can reread a bit you've misunderstood. Furthermore, your mental state when reading an exam paper is likely to be less relaxed and, therefore, you are more likely to read into a question what you expect or would like to be there rather than what is *actually* there. You may well be expecting, or even hoping, that a specific topic will crop up. Misreading what the examiner wants is all too easy under such circumstances. You would be surprised at the number of times pre-prepared answers have been written to questions which have *not* been asked. It is very common, but it should not be, if you tackle your exams with the sort of care described here.

▼

OK. I can accept your general point, but it's still all a bit vague. Can't you get down to some specific details?

Yes. No problem. Let's look at a very common error in the question-and-answer situation. Television quizzes. These are often riddled with inaccuracies.

Most of us have witnessed quizzes where the question-master has asked, 'Who can spell PARALLEL?' (or some other word). A buzzer sounds and a contestant proceeds to spell out 'P, A, R, A, L, L, E, L'. 'Correct,' says the questionmaster, 'full marks.' Actually, the answer is *totally incorrect*! Not the spelling. The answer. The correct answer to the question which was *asked* is, 'I can.' The question was 'Who can spell . . . ?' *not* 'What is the correct way to spell . . . ?' The actual spelling of the word is a different question altogether.

This may sound very pedantic, but when it comes to examinations, such distinctions can make all the difference between passing and failing. Examinations are not like TV quiz games. They are a serious matter and need to be treated as such.

▼

Right then, now I know what you have been getting at. That stuff about spelling was an example of a trick question, wasn't it?

Not really, but since you have brought the subject up, let us have a closer look at what you call 'trick questions'.

As I have stressed throughout this book, examiners are not ogres trying to trip up candidates. All they are trying to do is to establish whether the students have benefited sufficiently from the tuition received. If you can demonstrate that this is the case, then you pass. Remember also that an examiner would be being unfair if he were to pass a candidate who wasn't really up to the standard. If such a student were to move up to, say, the next year of a course, then he or she would be struggling even more than before, and the likelihood of success would be even slimmer because he/she hadn't really come to grips with the more basic knowledge.

Having said all that, the point about 'trick questions' has to be clarified. Obviously, television quizzes are basically for entertainment and a little latitude in accuracy is acceptable. In exams, precise terminology is essential if the examiner is to mark the papers fairly. It would be grossly unfair if an examiner had to award identical marks to two totally different answers simply because the examiner himself had made the question ambiguous. Good examiners don't do this. Their questions can be interpreted in one way and one way only.

▼

That doesn't sound right. You mean that every candidate has to answer the same question in the same way?

Of course not. I didn't say *answered* in one way, I said

interpreted in only one way. Perhaps it would be best if I gave you an example.

People often talk in a very lax, inaccurate manner. They don't always say exactly what they mean, but other people usually understand the general meaning. Lately, I saw a petrol lorry stopped by a pedestrian who drew the attention of the driver to the fact that a pipe was not secured, but was trailing on the road surface. The pedestrian said to the driver, 'Your pipe is trailing on the floor.' He didn't mean *floor* at all, of course, he meant the road surface, but everyone concerned understood what was meant.

Such laxity would never be acceptable in an examination. It would be utterly misleading. The answer to the question, 'What hazards would be involved if petrol were to be spilt on a floor?' would be totally different from the answer if the word 'floor' was replaced by 'ground' or 'road surface'.

The true meaning of what people say is usually derived from the *context* of what they are saying. Even the word 'floor' can mean different things in different contexts. It does not necessarily mean a surface covered with wooden floorboards. It could refer to the floor of a cave, the sea bed or a part of a legislative assembly (where a person with the right to speak is said to have been 'given the floor').

▼

OK. I accept that precise wording is essential and I'll be much more careful when I read the questions in future, but you are dodging the issue. You still haven't explained about trick questions.

Candidates for exams sometimes tend to think of examiners as the 'enemy'. They feel that examiners are out to trick them into making mistakes. This is simply not true. The idea of 'trick questions' results from candidates not reading the questions carefully enough, or, in some cases, examiners asking a question which is legitimate,

---

A Little Test – Just for Fun!

Read the following passage *once only*.

You are driving a bus with twenty-five passengers on board. At the first stop five passengers get off and ten get on. At the next stop, twelve passengers get on and four get off. Two get on at the next stop and six get off. At the next three stops, a total of ten passengers get off and four get on. The bus then reaches the terminus where everybody gets off.

Now answer the questions on page 145.

---

but not expected. There is no point in trying to 'trick' candidates. The examiner is not expecting perfection, just a *sufficient* knowledge and understanding of the subject.

We talked earlier in this chapter about rehearsing specific answers to questions which you think might appear on the paper. An unexpected question may still contain enough identifiable (expected) words to lead the candidate into the easy route of using the rehearsed answer.

These are not 'trick questions', they are simply misunderstandings on the part of the student.

▼

What you are saying, then, is that every word in an exam paper has been chosen very carefully and can have only one meaning. There can be no room for misunderstanding, if I read the paper carefully enough.

Precisely. There is one more thing that I might add, too. When you write something down, you know exactly what you mean. Other people may not, but you do. In the same way, there may be a very rare occasion when an examiner produces a question which can be answered in more than one way. If this happens, any candidate who gives a correct answer will be awarded the appropriate marks – even if the answer is not the one which the examiner expected. (Personally, in such a case, I would fail the examiner for being ambiguous!)

▼

All right, I'll accept what you say, but I'm still not convinced that errors in reading the paper can be all that big.

Believe me, it is true, but perhaps it will be easier to convince you with another example.

Let us take a hypothetical question on driving: 'Describe the sequence of actions which a good driver would perform when driving off from a stationary position.' Sounds simple enough. The answer would contain reference to depressing the clutch pedal, engaging first gear, depressing the accelerator while simultaneously releasing the clutch slowly and steering the car in the intended direction as it moves. No problem.

Now let us see what happens if we change just one word. Let us change 'stationary' to 'parked'. Not much difference, you might think, but let us think more deeply about it.

In a parked position, the engine will not be running; the mirror must be used to discover whether it is safe to move off; the indicator should be used to show the intention to move off and each of these points will need to be mentioned.

▼

Now I see what you've been driving at (sorry!). The 'stationary' position could have meant waiting at traffic lights, in a traffic jam or even queuing to get into a car park. There are about twice as many things to describe if you are moving off from a 'parked' position, so, presumably, there are twice as many marks to be gained. Now all your comments about careful reading are beginning to

Without referring back to page 143, answer the following questions.

1. What did you think this question would be?
Comment Most people will say that they expected the question to be 'How many people got off the bus?' Obviously, this was not the question, but you probably *expected* it to be, and, therefore, prepared to answer it. In other words, once the question had been anticipated, most (if not all) of your attention would be concentrated on this aspect of the text.

No marks, therefore, if you expected that the number 29 was going to be the answer to question 1. (You *did* remember that *everybody* got off – and that included the driver – didn't you?) Now try the next one.

2. How many stops did the bus make?
Comment Most people will get this one correct – with a bit of thought. After the last question, you've been primed, of course, and you included the last stop at the terminus. Good. Now for the next question.

3. What was the name of the driver?
Comment No. Don't laugh. You *have* been given all the information needed, although very few people will be able to answer this one. If you couldn't, the reason is that you were *expecting* to be asked about the number of alighting passengers and this prompted you to concentrate on that particular aspect of the text. Therefore you disregarded what appeared to be surplus information. Go back to the text to discover the correct answer.

OK, you could possibly claim that this has been a set of trick questions, and, up to a point, I will admit that it has been. However, I hope that you will have accepted some very important points which I have been trying to make about *anticipating* questions.

One last word. Seriously, *now* will you believe me when I say 'read the exam paper *carefully*'? – *and* more than once, if necessary!

make much more sense. But there is one thing that bothers me and that is what if I don't understand the meaning of the terms used on the paper?

That depends on the sort of 'terms' you are referring to. We can divide 'terms', or words, into two separate categories. Firstly, if you are referring to specific terms used in the subject, such as scientific terms, then you *ought* to know them. That is a fundamental part of what the subject, and the examination, is about. For example, the terms 'neutral', 'reciprocal' and 'sharp' have very specific meanings in Chemistry, Mathematics and Music respectively, so students of those subjects should be aware of what they mean and be able to write about them. On the other hand, the *same* terms would have very different meanings in the context of Politics, International Agreements and Domestic Science respectively. In other words, if the 'terms' you are referring to could be grouped under the general heading of 'definitions' (within the subject being examined), then the examiner will expect you to be aware of their meanings and to be able to demonstrate this in your answers.

▼

You said that there were two types of terms, though. What are the others?

The second category of 'terms' are those used in virtually all examinations. By this I mean terms such as 'list', 'describe', 'explain', 'compare and contrast' and so on. These words can also give rise to misunderstandings and, consequently, they need to be dealt with in some detail. This is done in Appendix 1, which contains an explanation of the more common terms.

▶ Summary ◀

1. Don't rush into answering the first question which seems 'easy'.
2. Give yourself sufficient time to read *all* the paper.

3. Don't forget to read the rubric.
4. Read *every* question on the paper before starting to write your answers.
5. Don't assume that you know what the question asks for. Reread the questions if necessary, until you are *sure* of the meaning (the only 'trick' questions are those which candidates misunderstand or don't expect).
6. Be sure that you recognise and understand 'definitions' and similar terms which are specific to the subject being examined.

Chapter 11

▼

Answering the Questions

I have answered three questions, and that is enough.
Lewis Carroll

Don't you believe it!
Brian Duncalf

Long before you actually see the examination paper, you will have a good idea about the topic areas which you are likely to avoid and, more importantly, the ones on which you are likely to gain a high score. There is nothing unusual in this as virtually everyone has likes and dislikes. Very few people are equally happy with all aspects of a given subject, even those to whom the subject is a favourite or specialism. The important thing is to realise that you are not alone in disliking some aspects of a subject and, therefore, you are not at a disadvantage compared to others taking the same examination, because they all feel the same way that you do! It cannot be stressed strongly enough how much difference your mental state, or confidence, can make to your performance in the examination. Think positively and you will win! If you don't believe this, then Chapter 12 should prove the point beyond any reasonable doubt.

Right then, back to the exam paper. You have read the question paper, perhaps twice, and maybe read one or two questions a third time in order to make quite sure what is really wanted of you. You have taken your time (as advised in Chapter 10) to let your subconscious work

100 per cent Memory – 100 per cent Marks?

'But I've worked hard and learned my lessons well,' complained a student who had failed to reach a satisfactory score in one examination. He even produced his lecture notes and showed me all the points which he had mentioned in what he thought was his best answer. His performance on that question was his worst of the whole paper.

On referring to his exam script later I discovered that his answer was identical to his lecture notes. He had a 'photographic memory' and he had used it!

The examination was at a very high academic level and the question concerned the structure of a colour slide film and its reaction to exposure and processing when the exposure had taken place accidentally through the back of the film, rather than conventionally. Any candidate who understood the basic principles would have been able to answer the question easily and, in fact, the rest of the students in his group scored very high marks on the question.

To all intents and purposes what the student was saying to the examiner was, 'I know all the information needed to answer this question is in there somewhere. You sort out the important bits and you put them together to find the answer.' You can imagine a busy examiner's response to this!

It is not unlike a busy executive asking his new secretary to find a telephone number for him and, in response, having a directory thrown on his desk with the comment, 'Sure. It's in there.' (Such a secretary would be well advised to find the location of the nearest Social Security Office!)

on the material in your memory, and you have composed yourself to tackle the job in hand.

The best way to tackle the paper is to select, carefully, the question on which you think you will give your best performance. If you have done your revision properly, then you should find yourself saying something like, 'That's an easy one. I didn't expect a give-away as simple as that', or, at least, 'That's not too bad, I can make a decent job of that one.' That question is the one which you should attempt first.

There are advantages in taking this line of attack. One is that you will occupy your mind so completely that any question of 'nerves' should disappear. You will be so busy writing that you won't realise that there is anything to worry or be nervous about. You will be scoring marks on the paper virtually without knowing it.

Another advantage about tackling your best topic first is that it will put your mind in a more positive state. Once you have started to set your thoughts down on paper, you may well find yourself wishing that there was more time. You will be different from ill-prepared candidates who will be waiting for the time when they can get out of the examination room because they have insufficient to say in their answers.

Having touched upon the subject of time, it is worthwhile dealing with it in more detail, as there are good ways and bad ways of using your time in the examination room.

▶ Tackling Your First Question ◀

When you have found a question on which you think you can score a high mark, it is very easy to fall into the trap of spending too much time on it in the hope that your score will be higher still. It seems a logical step, but it doesn't quite work out that way. Here's why.

Let us take an imaginary situation in order to explain a point of principle. Again let me restate that it does not matter whether or not the example given here corresponds to the sort of question or question paper which you will encounter in practice. What *does* matter is the

Getting the 'Nasties' out of the Way

Some people, when faced with a number of chores which they must perform, choose the one which they dislike the most to tackle first. They get this one out of the way and then move on to a slightly less onerous task. In this way, they get the nasty ones over quickly and finish their chores on a high note.

The technique has much to commend it, *but not in the case of answering examination questions.*

There are two reasons for not adopting this method in your exams. Firstly, you should try to keep your spirits as high as possible from the outset and this cannot be done by attempting a question with which you are not too happy. You need to tackle your *best* question first.

The second reason for taking this line of attack is that, providing you have a choice of questions, it should not be necessary to attempt the worst question at all!

All this seems to be common sense, but, over the years, I have known a number of ill-advised students who have fallen into that trap. Make sure that *you* don't do it.

principle involved. Numbers, scores and other details can all be adjusted to suit your particular situation. What I am using here is an example, nothing more.

Imagine a question which is worth twenty marks. Let us suppose that it is an essay type of question and that the examiner is going to be looking for twenty facts and comments, each of which will score one point. In other words, if you make appropriate comments on twenty of the required facts, then you will score full marks for that particular question. That sounds like a good start and if you manage it then you will be well on the way to reaching the pass mark for the whole examination. Remember this when you read Chapter 12, because reference will be made to it.

Now, before we go any further, let us look at the likelihood of gaining those twenty marks. We will assume that if you remember a relevant fact, then you will also remember enough information to comment on that fact and score its corresponding one mark. Therefore, the issue is really about remembering those twenty facts. Again, the subject of remembering lists of facts has been dealt with in Chapter 7, but let us work on the assumption that you haven't (in this case) used any mnemonics or memory aids. Instead you are simply going to try to recall and make suitable comments on twenty facts.

If you think about it, the first (say) five facts should be easy to remember. Practically anybody can recall five items from a list of twenty – after all, this is the equivalent of remembering only one item from a list of four. OK?

This means that the first five marks for that particular question are as good as guaranteed! It would be very difficult to prove that you can't score those first five marks (providing, of course, that you have revised adequately).

Earning the next *ten* marks takes rather more effort, because the list of facts to be recalled is getting smaller. Even so, the next five marks should not be too difficult (it's still only one item out of three) so that a score of ten marks (out of the total twenty) should be well within your reach.

The mark for point eleven has to be recalled from the list of ten remaining, the mark for point twelve from the list of nine remaining, the thirteenth mark from a list of eight, and so on. The more items you remember, the more difficult it will be to recall the remaining ones from the diminishing number available.

The natural result of all this is that the *last* five marks are going to be the most difficult to score, as you will have to remember five facts out of five. Not so easy!

It will, however, be very easy to score the *first* five

marks on the *next* question. Much easier than scoring those last five marks on the original question.

The lesson to be learned is, therefore, not to spend an excessive amount of time on any single question on the paper. This is particularly true if giving a full answer to any specified question will result in your having insufficient time to answer, in full, another question later. Obviously, the technique to adopt is to time your answers!

▶ Timing your Answers ◀

Having read the paper carefully and ascertained what *precisely* is wanted of you (as described in Chapter 10), then look at how much time is left for you to answer the whole paper. As stressed in Chapter 10, plenty of time should be given to reading the exam paper fully. Ten to fifteen minutes for a three-hour paper is not excessive.

So, suppose that you have an exam paper of three hours' duration. You are expected to answer five questions from a total of (say) eight or nine. Let us suppose that you spend a quarter of an hour reading the paper. That leaves two and three-quarter hours or 165 minutes in which to put all your answers down on paper. Divided between the five questions, this gives you thirty-three minutes per question. Round this figure down to thirty minutes and you have a basis on which to tackle the full examination, i.e. a quarter of an hour reading the paper, two and a half hours to be spent answering each of five questions (half an hour each) and a quarter of an hour 'spare'. We'll come to that so-called spare time later.

▶ Spending your Time Efficiently ◀

Having established our plan of campaign, let us now look into the method of approaching each question.

The initial reading of the paper has indicated your 'best' question, i.e. the one on which you are likely to gain the highest score. We have already established that this is the one to tackle first.

Mathematical Questions

There are occasions when a mathematical question is set in an otherwise non-mathematical examination. Such a question offers the well-prepared student an opportunity to excel. What is not generally realised is that it is possible to gain almost full marks on these questions, even when the final 'answer' is wrong!

The examiner assumes a suitable mathematical ability on the part of the candidate, but these questions are intended to test the *understanding* of some principle or other. In other words, the candidate is given certain pieces of information from which he is expected to derive conclusions, formulae or some other result. Given the data 'A', the candidate is expected to calculate the next item 'B', followed by 'C', 'D' and so on. The mathematical content is, therefore, a means to an end and not the end itself. It follows that, if a mathematical error is introduced early in the calculation, then the final 'answer' is bound to be wrong, even though the correct procedures have been applied. However, as it is the *procedure* which is being examined (not the Maths) then full marks can be gained *for the procedure*, but a small penalty (and only a small penalty) will have to be paid for a small mathematical error.

While writing about your favourite question (if there is such a thing as a 'favourite' question!), you will probably find that time is running out quickly – after all, the question was your first choice. As the thirty minutes allocation comes up you must make a positive decision. Do you carry on with the current question or do you move on to the next one? Here's what you do.

Ask yourself how far you have gone with this particular

answer. Half way? Three-quarters? Or have you almost finished?

If you have almost finished, then carry on, but don't go *too* far past the thirty-minute period. A couple of minutes is OK. Even five – remember that 'spare' fifteen minutes? But don't go over the five-minute mark. Finish off the question after that period of time and get on with the next question.

You may object to this advice on the basis that you are short-changing yourself on your best question. That may or may not be true, but remember that the *last* five marks (of twenty) are the most difficult ones to score. You will be better advised to score the more easily obtainable five marks on the next question.

Another point comes in here also. You have rationed your time to give equal periods to each question. But the likelihood is that, by the time that you have reached the last question, the amount of time you need to answer it will be somewhat shorter than the thirty minutes you have allotted. After all, the last question is the *worst* one of your choice, so you may not need as much time as you needed for the first one, because you may not have as much to say. If this is not true, i.e. if you need as much time to answer the last question as the first (and if you are answering them satisfactorily), then you need not concern yourself too much with squeezing those extra few points – you will already have scored a more-than-adequate mark to pass the exam! There again, you may be aiming at more than a mere pass mark. In which case, we will pursue our exam strategy a bit further.

▶ **Some Finer Points on Timing** ◀

So far, we have looked at answering your 'best' question, but haven't decided what to do if you run out of the allocated time and before you have completed the answer.

If you have only completed (say) half of the answer, then there is something wrong with your answering

The Price of 'Padding'

You are picking up your groceries when you notice a few items which you did not order. Some smoked salmon, caviare and, perhaps, a bottle of expensive champagne. All good stuff, of course, but definitely *not* on the shopping list which you left the previous day.

'I'm not paying for that,' you protest. 'You can leave it in the basket if you like, but I'm not paying for it.'

Quite right, too. No reasonable person can expect you to pay for goods which you have not ordered.

Your examiner also has a 'shopping list'. It's in the form of items asked for in each question. You provide him with the goods, and he pays you the price in the form of the corresponding marks for your answer. But by the same rule, if you give him material which he has not asked for, he won't pay you with the marks. It may all be good, accurate, academic stuff, but if it isn't on the examiner's 'shopping list', then he doesn't even *have* the marks available to give you.

There *is* a price to pay though, and *you* pay it. It's in the form of time, precious time, which should have been used to give answers to questions actually asked, and for which marks have been allocated on the examiner's marking scheme.

The lesson is simple. Don't 'waffle' or pad out your answers. If you can't answer a part of a question with relevant information, then get on with answering a part of another question for which marks *are* available. *That* is the way to pass exams!

technique. You have probably been waffling. Don't do it. Padding out answers fills paper, but it doesn't win marks.

Perhaps you are only approximately three-quarters of the way through your answer. In which case your best bet is to start the next question. The reason for this should be obvious by now, but may still benefit from further explanation.

Assuming that the material you have put down in answer to the question is satisfactory, then answering three-quarters of the question is likely to produce three-quarters of the marks allocated to that question. Even if this is not the case, your score is still likely to be a substantial one. Certainly enough to reach a 'pass' on that question.

It has been stated elsewhere that examiners are not looking for opportunities to fail candidates. They will give a candidate the benefit of the doubt, if the candidate gives them the opportunity. If you have spent thirty minutes answering the question asked, and if you have been writing sensibly about the subject, then you must have shown the examiner that you know a substantial amount about it.

In most cases, an examiner is not looking for mere repetition of a list of facts (a well-trained parrot could probably do that!) – what he wants is an indication of your *understanding* of the subject material. The more you write, the more you give the examiner the opportunity to see whether you understand the subject and the more he is likely to give you the benefit of the doubt. This assumes that your answer is not 'padded out' with lots of irrelevant material, of course.

So, you have answered your first question and you are now selecting the second. Choose the one with which you are next happiest. Perhaps there are two questions with which you feel equally at ease. In which case tackle either of them, and move on to the other as your third answer.

▶ The 'End-Game' of the Paper ◀

After you have answered four questions, you will have used up something in the order of 80 per cent of the examination time, and you should have ensured that you have not less than thirty minutes for your last question.

As far as that last question is concerned, you could be in one of two predicaments. Firstly, and this is often the case, you may have to choose the 'best of a bad bunch' and, in this event, the choice should probably be made by eliminating, progressively, the questions with which you are least happy. Eventually, you will reach the question with which you are most likely (out of the 'bad bunch') to score the highest mark possible under the circumstances.

Alternatively, you may be in the fortunate position of having two or more questions with which you are equally happy. Well, you will be fortunate in some respects. You do have a greater choice. However, you also have the disadvantage of having to choose one question from an equally desirable two. One thing you must *not* do under these circumstances is attempt both questions!

In order to understand the reasons for not answering more questions than the number asked for by the examiner, it is necessary to appreciate the way in which examination papers are marked.

For the sake of simplicity, we will still keep to our specimen structure of five questions to be answered from eight, with twenty marks for each question. Consequently, the total number of marks available for the whole examination paper will be one hundred – this corresponds to 100 per cent. Now, when marking the paper, the examiner will mark each question in turn, and record the mark for each. When five have been answered, the number of marks will be totalled. (More often than not, you will see a box on the front page of the answer book printed for the convenience of the examiner to record the marks for each question, and the total. Usually, you will be asked to fill in the numbers of the questions you have answered, in the order in which you have answered them. Always be sure to do this, not only for the benefit of the examiner but also, and in some ways more importantly, for your own benefit. It represents a quick and convenient way for *you* to check that you have answered the required number of questions.)

Again, for the sake of simplicity, suppose that you have answered the required five questions and scored ten marks for each question. That all comes to a total of fifty marks or 50 per cent – which, incidentally, will usually mean you have passed.

Now suppose that you decide to answer a *sixth* question. What we should really ask is, *why*? Do you expect to gain more marks? You won't! The examiner will add up the total marks for *five* of the questions and stop there. He (or she) knows that the first five marks of the sixth question will be easier to score than the last five marks of the fifth, but those other five marks (of one of the six questions) will be ignored. If the examiner wants you to answer only five questions then he (or she) will allow you to score marks on *only* five questions.

Similar arguments apply to answering a little of *all* of the questions on the paper. You may be able to score the easy first five marks on all eight questions on the paper, but you will not gain forty marks on the paper as a whole. You will only score twenty-five marks, five marks for each of the five questions which the examiner accepts.

Another point to be taken into account is that, if you answer a sixth question, you will really be wasting time. The time spent on the sixth question would be much better spent on one or more of the first five.

You may think that you could gain some advantage by answering a sixth question because you might score more marks on the sixth question than on one or other of the previous five. This argument is only partially valid.

It is true that an examiner will mark *all* the questions answered and he will add up the five *highest* scores (as I've said before, examiners *are* fair!). Hence, theoretically, the sixth question could possibly gain a higher score than one of the previous five. However, when you consider the *time* taken to answer that sixth question (it could be fifteen minutes or even more) it should be evident that those extra minutes would have been better spent checking one or more of the previous five, looking for omissions, say, or making sure what you have written

Running out of Time

The importance of timing of your answers cannot be over-emphasised and, all things being equal, you should always be in charge of this aspect of your exam. Nevertheless, examination candidates do occasionally misjudge matters and, for one reason or another, find that time is running out faster than they had anticipated. If this happens, what should you do?

For reasons explained elsewhere in this chapter, *under no circumstances* should you omit a question. Instead, make the best of whatever time is available and tackle that last question. (It should go without saying that an error of judgement *may* leave you with insufficient time to answer a *single* question, but it is totally inexcusable to allow yourself to be so short of time that you risk missing out more than one.) Rushing an answer to the last question should be avoided. Instead, make a list of the topics that you would like to include in your answer. Do this in a conspicuous manner so that the examiner can see it. Then make brief notes on *every* item on the list. After that, use whatever time is left to amplify the notes. This technique will enable the examiner to judge the extent of your knowledge of the topic, and you will be awarded marks accordingly.

is what you want to say. After all, those five are your *best* five. You know more about those topics and are likely, therefore, to gain a higher score with those than with any others.

A further point needs to be raised here. If you have done your revision properly and allocated your time in the exam sensibly, you shouldn't have enough time to tackle a sixth question. You should have been too busy answering your best five. OK, sometimes you run 'dry' when answering exam questions, that is, you temporarily run out of information which you really need to complete a good answer. This is not uncommon, especially under examination conditions. However, it is another reason for adequate timing of your answers.

Again, it will be of benefit to see how exam papers are set and marked. The examiner knows how much information he is asking for and he also knows, fairly accurately, how much time will be needed to write that information on the paper. All this has been allowed for in setting the paper. So, if you spend ten minutes answering a question for which twenty or twenty-five minutes have been allowed, then, obviously, you have missed something out!

There is no need to worry, though. If you remember, at the beginning of this chapter, I suggested that you ration your time to give an equal amount to each of the questions you answer. This should have appeared to be logical enough then, but there is a bonus. *If* you have given short measure to one, or more, questions, then at the end of your time spent writing, you will have enough time left to go over your answers again and this could have considerable value in more ways than one.

As I stated in Chapter 10, the brain is capable of doing many things simultaneously and without our being aware of it, so that, just as when you were originally reading the exam paper, reading over your answers will also serve to bring into focus some material which may have been overlooked when you were writing. It is possible, for example, that you have missed out a whole section of a multi-part question. This happens quite often. After giving a good and thorough answer to a well-understood question, it is possible to become so elated with success that you rush into the next question, overlooking the fact that there is a second part to the first one.

The warning sign that all is not as well as it should be is having too much time left over at the end of the exam. The answer? Read through your script. Don't take too much time over this. You don't need to. You know what you have said and it is not so much what you have said that is important at this time. It is what you have *not* said!

You should also read through the questions themselves, to check that there is nothing you have missed. The omission of a whole section of a multi-part question will be easy to spot, and, for that matter, easy to rectify. But what if several facts have been missed out from an answer? Three things. Firstly, don't panic! Secondly, marshal your thoughts on the information that you have omitted. Get what you want to say clear in your mind. Finally, make some mark such as an asterisk or star at the point in your answer where you wish to add more information. Any sort of symbol will do as long as it will bring the examiner's attention to that point. Then at some convenient place, such as in the margin of the paper, write something like 'continued on page XX' or 'continued on separate sheet number YY', whatever the page number may be.

All you are trying to do here is draw the attention of the examiner to the fact that you have not finished your answer on the current page, but have completed it elsewhere. You will not be penalised for this. In fact, an examiner will be pleased to see that you have been systematic in presenting your answer, and, with it, you will have made his job of marking your paper easier.

▶ Don't gamble! ◀

Before proceeding any further, an important point needs to be made. As I said earlier, examiners, given the opportunity, will give you the benefit of any doubts. But *only* if you have given sufficient information to enable them to do this. This does not mean that you can gamble with their generous attitude. You may feel that, if you have some doubts about a particular aspect of a subject, offering two alternative answers will ensure that you score for the correct one. Forget it! This will do nothing but demonstrate to the examiner that you are unsure about the subject and are trying to hedge your bets in order to get the answer right. In his place, what would you do? Yes, give marks for neither. Under these circumstances, an examiner will never give you the benefit of the doubt, because you don't deserve it.

▶ Changing your Answers ◀

It sometimes happens that, under the strain of examination conditions, you need to revise an answer or even alter it totally. There is no harm in this *providing that* you make it quite clear that you have altered your answer. In other words, if, after rereading your script, you feel a part of an answer is ambiguous or even wrong, *cross it out*. Make no mistake about this and leave the examiner under no illusion about it either. You will not be penalised. Rewrite the correct answer (or part of it, as appropriate) and let the examiner see that this revision of your answer is what you intend him to mark you on. Once again, it may be necessary to put this revised answer in a different part of the answer book, or even on a separate sheet. This does not matter as long as you make it clear to the examiner where the corrected part of your answer can be found. This is not only logical, it is also a courtesy to the examiner. Remember, he may have to mark dozens, even hundreds, of scripts. One way to frustrate an examiner is to make him waste his time looking around your answer book for bits of answers that may, or there again may not, be there. This is hardly the way to win friends and influence examiners! For *your* sake, make the examiner's job as easy as possible. It will do you no harm and will probably do you a lot of good. (If you think that answering an exam paper is a chore, just think what a chore marking a multitude of exam papers must be!)

▶ Unequally Weighted Questions ◀

So far, we have worked on the assumption that every question on the exam paper has been allotted the same

Part Questions

Occasionally it is possible to be put off-balance with a part question. The sort of thing I am referring to is the question which starts off with 'Name *three* . . .' (The items could be sauces containing a specified ingredient, components of an electrical circuit or artists of the Renaissance period – the details don't matter here.)

If you know the answers, then obviously there is nothing to worry about, but what if you are taken totally unawares, without the vaguest idea of an answer? There is still little need to worry. The examiner has a vast amount of material from which to ask such questions and it may well be that you simply haven't revised (or even come across) this information.

The important point to remember is that if you are being asked for three *names*, then the marks allocated are likely to be only three in total. After all, remembering three names is no more than a feat of *memory* – it does not mean that you necessarily know anything about the subject.

Regard such part questions as a means of gaining bonus marks, rather than the whole crux of the question. Whatever you do, do not allow yourself to be put at a disadvantage by the sight of an introduction to a question such as this. Remember, the majority of marks are going to be gained from answering the *rest* of the question (for which, incidentally, you may be well prepared).

number of marks and this is often the case. However, what happens on those other occasions when it is not? Usually the marks that can be gained from individual questions will be indicated on the question paper and, of course, the time spent on these questions ought to be adjusted accordingly. However, such papers will normally contain questions of *approximately* the same value so that complex calculations dealing with time should not be necessary.

When questions are arranged in two or more sections and if the corresponding marks are not indicated, then allocating your time should not be a problem: you can safely assume that every part question will carry the same marks, so it is easy to work out how much time to spend on each.

Another way of subdividing questions is to ask for a list of general facts, followed by details on some or all of them. A simple list might carry one mark for each name or point. The bulk of the marks will be gained from the more demanding task of writing detailed comments about the items on the list. Your time should be allocated accordingly.

▶ Multiple-Choice Questions ◀

Everything that has been mentioned so far has dealt with questions requiring an essay type of answer. Multiple-choice questions are very different in nature and the method of tackling them is also different.

This type of paper does not necessitate the sort of precision in the recollection of facts that essay questions do, nor, of course, does it require you to have great skills of self-expression. The correct answers are already on the exam paper and all that is required of you is to identify them.

It is not necessary for you to read through the whole paper (or a multiple-choice section) in order to determine the questions which you are going to answer. Usually you are required to answer *all* of them! This, at least, removes the need to select questions to be answered.

Another point is that, although the role of memory is reduced, multiple-choice does not absolve you of the need to know your subject. In theory, if you have to choose one possible answer from four offered, you have a one-in-four chance of selecting the correct answer, at least from the standpoint of statistics. In theory, therefore, you should be able to score 25 per cent, even if you know nothing whatsoever about the subject! However, to pass such an exam, you will normally need to score a higher mark than with the essay type of question, otherwise the whole point of the examination will be cancelled out.

The last comment to be made here is that, if you have to answer every question, you may as well go through the whole exam paper (or multiple-choice section) from beginning to end and answer the questions as they arise. There is little to be gained by doing anything else. So, after reading the general requirements at the top of the exam paper carefully, move on to the first question and indicate which answer you believe to be the correct one. But supposing the first question has you stumped? What do you do? Simple. Don't waste time on it, but move on to the next question. As mentioned in Chapter 10, your subconscious will be working on that first question while you are answering the others. It may be that while you are answering some other question, the answer to question 1 will come to the forefront of your memory and it will be an easy matter to go back and place your mark against the correct answer. Or it may be that, for whatever reason, you can't produce the answer. If that is the case then don't worry and don't waste time. Get on with the job of scoring marks on the questions which you *can* answer.

Once you have answered the 'easy' questions, you can then go over the whole paper again and try to complete the questions which you missed originally. However, make sure that you use the same technique of not wasting time on questions which require a lot of thought. That comes next.

Providing you have used your time efficiently, there should be some minutes left to do some deep thinking; even if there are not, you will have done as much as you

Cheating

The vast majority of examination candidates accept exams for what they are, a means of testing the knowledge and understanding of the work on the course. However, every year a few candidates are disqualified because of cheating. It's quite stupid to try to use unfair means, but it happens. Often.

A fact, or series of facts, that can be recorded on a piece of paper can just as easily be recorded in the memory – the brain has a far greater capacity than any piece of paper, or any portable computer for that matter.

What potential cheats seem to overlook is the psychological pressure involved in the *thought* of using unfair methods. Waiting for opportunities to read the contents of hidden pieces of paper (or to use whatever other method may be employed) interferes with the process of answering the questions and, under examination conditions, candidates need to be as relaxed as possible and to use their time as efficiently as possible.

In other words, the time and effort spent in preparing to cheat would be infinitely better spent in more conventional preparation.

could under the circumstances. This is the way to maximise your efforts. However, if there is some time left, then there is another technique for you to adopt.

Suppose that you have a question to which you think you *should* know the answer. You have (say) four alternatives from which to choose. Right, then. If you don't know the correct answer, eliminate the *incorrect* ones. At first sight, it should be obvious that one of the alternatives is quite incorrect. Make a mental note of it. Continue the process until you have eliminated three, and the one remaining must be the correct one. It is as simple as that.

Finally, even if you can't eliminate three of the four possible answers, then eliminating only two (or even one) will still improve your chances of selecting the right answer. After all, if you eliminate two answers, then there's a fifty-fifty chance of your picking the correct answer by accident!

▶ Presentation ◀

Presentation is often overlooked where examinations are concerned, but it is important.

Make sure that your pen doesn't leak. A script with ink blotches all over it looks a mess and does not impress your examiner. It may seem a small point, but you should still take care of it.

On the subject of pens, make sure that you have a spare one (and that it is in good working order). It can be most frustrating to have to break off while in the full flood of answering a question and it may well also break your concentration.

Another way in which examiners can be adversely affected is by being presented with an exam script full of tightly packed, spidery writing. Make sure that your writing is legible – there is no point in getting your answers correct if the examiner can't read them! Also, paper is not rationed during examinations, so use as much as you need. Parts of answers which are changed or added to after the main one (see pages 162–163) are probably best put on a separate sheet. This makes the whole process easier for you to write, and for the examiner to mark.

Finally, take care over spelling and punctuation. It may not seem very major to you, but spelling *is* important. In fact, in many exams it is automatic for candidates to be penalised for spelling errors. The answer to this is straightforward (and I don't mean that you should take a dictionary into the examination room). Simply take more care during term time! Get into the habit of spelling properly when your time is not at a premium. Do the same with your punctuation. After all, as they say, if a job is worth doing at all, then it's worth doing properly (*and* the first time).

▶ Summary ◀

1. From the information in the rubric, assess the amount of time available for each question (take into account any unequally weighted questions).
2. Answer your 'best' question first, followed by 'next bests'.
3. Ration your time for answering each question and do not exceed the time allowed.
4. Do not answer more questions than necessary – you will be wasting time.
5. Stick to the question *as asked* and do not 'pad out' your answers with irrelevant information.
6. As soon as you have finished answering a question, record the number of the question in the box provided on the answer book. This will give *you* a record of your progress.
7. If you are running short of time on your last question, make a list and brief notes on what you *would have written* in answer to the question. The examiner will be able to award marks for this.
8. If you have any time to spare after answering your last question, use it to check that you have answered everything required of you. Any material to be added to your script should be written and *clearly labelled* so that the examiner can locate it easily.
9. Answer multiple-choice questions straight away, but omit any which will cause problems. You can return to these later, time permitting.
10. Be as neat as possible with your answers. Ensure that your writing is legible and try to use correct spelling and grammar.
11. Don't try to cheat – it's a waste of everybody's time.

Chapter 12

▼

You can't possibly fail (unless you really want to!)

A minute's success pays the failure of years.
Robert Browning

If you have read this book through to this point, then you will be in one of two positions. Possibly you have not yet sat the examination and are wondering whether the effort is going to be worth it. Don't worry, you are not on your own. Most candidates feel like this. It is all too easy at this point to persuade yourself that you are likely to fail anyway. 'So-and-so is much better than me at this subject', 'I'm no good at this subject' or 'I'm hopeless at exams anyway, so I'm bound to fail' are all attitudes I've heard before – and there are dozens more, usually from students who passed the examination later, if not with flying colours, then at least with an ample margin. The real point is that your state of mind before an examination is hardly at its best, human beings being what they are. I can't stop you from worrying, only you can do that, but at least I can help you to get the situation into perspective (if Chapter 6 hasn't done this already).

The second possibility is that you have taken the paper and are in that all-too-familiar state, before the examination results are published, where each day seems like ten years; you've convinced yourself that you have failed; your fingernails have been bitten almost to the elbows and you have been sticking pins into wax effigies of all examiners, past and present. If this is the case, then forget it! All these worries are totally pointless and what you should be doing is getting on with the process of living, because everything that you can do has been done. You can't alter the outcome now.

In fact, there is not much point in reading this chapter *after* the examination, because the whole point is to show you how easy it is to pass.

Having said all that, let us now get down to the matter in hand, which is to show how adequate preparation and examination technique will virtually guarantee you a pass mark. The only proviso which I will make first is that you must be an *eligible* candidate for the examination (or examinations) you are to take. In effect, this means that the examination must be within your personal capabilities. Not everyone has the ability or necessary background to be a brain surgeon – or for that matter a bricklayer. A suitable candidate for one of these professions may be totally unsuitable for the other. But if your teacher, tutor or other mentor feels that your abilities are up to the challenge, or if you are so determined that you will allow nothing to stand in your way, then you *will* pass that exam.

Firstly, to assess your likely performance, we will have to consider the marks or scores which you are likely to obtain. Obviously, there are dozens of different types of question papers, each with their own form of marking, and it would be tedious, if not impossible, to attempt to survey them all. Hence I am going to set out a standard examination format which we can use as a yardstick. Don't worry if the format is not like the one which you are likely to encounter; again, it is the *principle* which matters, not the detail, and this principle can be modified to apply to any examination structure.

I am going to assume that the examination gives candidates a choice of questions. Let us assume that the examination paper contains seven or eight questions and that, for the convenience of the mathematics, candidates are required to answer five. This means that, if each

Failure can be in the mind

I went to an examination room to collect some scripts and was met by a small group of mature students. 'We've all failed. There's no point in going on,' they claimed. Their comments about the difficulty of the examination paper were derogatory, to put it mildly.

As the exam had been the first of four and they had another to sit after the lunch break, the situation was serious. Despite my reassurances, they would not be placated. They were going home because they were adamant that there was no point in taking any more exams.

Each member of the group was conscientious and capable, and there was the very real possibility of the whole year's work being put into jeopardy if they didn't continue with their exams. As my pleas went unheeded, I suggested that they went to the local pub, where I would meet them after I had locked their scripts away safely. They agreed.

About an hour (and several drinks!) later, their disappointment had mellowed somewhat and they accepted my argument that, having already done the preparation, they had little to lose by sitting the next examination, which I was to invigilate.

Every student passed the course and obtained the appropriate certification — but the situation could have been very different had they persisted with their original intention to give up after that first exam!

The moral should be self-evident.

question is allocated twenty marks, the total marks for all the questions answered can be expressed directly as a percentage. (I mention *answered* rather than *to be answered*, simply to restate the advice given in Chapter 11. Remember?)

Now let us look at the examination requirements. Many examinations require a mark of 40 per cent for a so-called pass. Of course, this figure varies depending upon the examining body, but 40 per cent is not uncommon. If the pass mark is higher, say 50 per cent, then allowances will be made, such as a larger choice of questions or a less strict standard of marking.

Now let us look at the subject of target scores. What do you consider to be a reasonable mark for set work carried out at your leisure – that is 'homework' or whatever you want to call it? If you had done your work well, then a score of five out of ten would hardly be considered satisfactory, don't you agree? Wouldn't seven be a more realistic figure, or better still eight? (If you are used to scoring nines and tens for the term's work, then that subject should give you very little cause for concern, and you probably don't need to be reading this bit.)

Now, let us translate that term's mark to an examination mark. Remember, the first question which you are going to answer on the paper is going to be your *best* answer. You can therefore expect your best mark. Just for the sake of argument, suppose you score eight out of ten for that question on the paper. That is the same as sixteen out of twenty. So far, so good. (No, don't say, 'But what if the score is smaller?' at this stage. I'll come to that later. Just assume that you score sixteen marks for your best answer.)

The second question which you answer will be your second best, so for the sake of argument, let us assume that you score the equivalent of seven out of ten – that is fourteen out of twenty on the examination paper. So far, this should not be regarded as excessively ambitious (again, if it is, we'll deal with it later – just bear with me for a while).

Let us now summarise the position. Your progress in the examination so far is:

	Score (individual)	Score (total as %)
First question	16	16
Second question	14	30

Right. So far your total score is 30 per cent. You are well within reach of that target 'pass' score of 40 per cent – and you've only answered two questions so far!

Now let us look at your third, fourth and fifth choice of question. Is it too much to ask for you to score three marks out of ten for your third question, perhaps another one (yes, *one*) for the fourth choice and another miserly one mark for your fifth question? Let's face it, if you can't do better than that, then you don't deserve to pass! If you can't achieve scores of this magnitude then you simply haven't done the preparation properly. You haven't followed the advice in this book.

Supposing that you *do* make these scores. They will correspond to six, two and two marks (out of twenty) on the paper. Your overall score is now:

	Score (individual)	Score (total as %)
First question	16	16
Second question	14	30
Third question	6	36
Fourth question	2	38
Fifth question	2	**40**

You've *passed*! You have scored that required 40 per cent. No problem.

OK, I know what you are going to say at this point (I've heard this one hundreds of times). 'But,' you claim, 'there's no way that I'm going to score sixteen out of twenty under examination conditions, and even that fourteen is a bit suspect.' All right, then, just suppose that you don't score sixteen (for your first choice, remember?). Is *six* out of ten too much to ask for the question on which you think you will perform your best?

How about a measly five out of ten for your second choice? Let us suppose that you are not going to do fantastically well with *any* question, but that you can perform moderately well on four out of the required five. Those scores mentioned above correspond to examination scores of twelve and ten respectively for your first and second questions. Obviously, you will have to do better on the other questions (but we are talking of better than three out of ten and one out of ten). Is that too much to ask? Can you manage four, three and two respectively for your third, fourth and fifth choice? These marks give you scores of eight, six and four out of twenty and your examination performance now looks like this:

	Score (individual)	Score (total as %)
First question	12	12
Second question	10	22
Third question	8	30
Fourth question	6	36
Fifth question	4	**40**

You have *still* passed – despite all your doubts! Satisfied yet?

The important thing to note is that you *must* answer the full number of questions required (as explained in Chapter 11).

Finally, any residual worries should be dispelled by the thought that, if you can't excel in any specific question, then all you need to do is to score eight marks (i.e. four marks out of ten) on each question, and you will still pass! Any score above this will be leading you on to a mark of greater credit. As I said at the beginning of this chapter, you can only fail if you really want to!

Finally, although it is true that a specific examination structure has been used as an example and that the examination which you are to take may be quite different, the same approach is just as applicable to any other examination structure and the same outcome is just as inevitable, i.e. if you've done the work properly, then you simply *can't fail*.

My last comments to you are not to wish you good luck in your examinations. Luck should have very little to do with it.

My final words are 'Good preparation!'

Appendix 1

▼

Terms Used in Examination Papers

I keep six honest serving men
They taught me all I knew:
Their names are What and Why and When
And How and Where and Who.

Rudyard Kipling

It should go without saying that, basically, examination papers consist of *questions*. The variety of questions appears to be infinite, but in fact they conform, more or less, to the six questions quoted above. Yes, they appear to be simple questions, and they are. However, you only have to listen to answers to questions on television interviews, for example, to realise that one person can answer a question with a single sentence, whereas another (perhaps a politician?) may take many minutes to answer the same question – and, perhaps, without really saying any more.

With examinations, candidates have no such latitude. Examiners have a series of standard terms which are used in examination question papers. These terms are quite specific in their meaning and there should be no room for ambiguity. When you read the paper, the examiner's requirements should be totally clear, and if they are not, then you should read the question again until the meaning *is* clear.

Obviously, it would be impractical to attempt to deal with all the words which could possibly be found in examination papers, but it should be of benefit to survey and comment on the more common ones.

In order to apply the following examples to as wide a field as possible, academic subjects will be avoided and, in their place, topics related more to everyday life will be used where practicable.

▶ List ◀

This term means exactly what it says. You will be expected to make a list of the items asked for. This is not particularly demanding: it requires little more than a good memory and, by and large, this is not really what examinations are all about! Such a question is intended to test the *general scope* of your knowledge of the subject material.

For this reason, it would be unwise to produce anything more than a simple list. There is no point in spending valuable time producing details that are not needed. If the examiner wants more information, he'll ask for it.

Variations on the 'list' theme include such instructions as 'list briefly' or 'list as fully as possible'. There is little room for confusion here, and your response should match the question asked.

Incidentally, it is advisable to record your list vertically: that way you can add to it later, if you find that you have omitted some important detail. This is less easy to do if your list is recorded across the page, with little space between each pair of items. This may seem to be common sense, but I have been presented with cramped horizontal lists on occasions. Another point: a vertical list not only enables the examiner to identify the individual items more easily, it helps *you* to do so when checking over your paper later.

Very occasionally you might be asked to list in decreasing (or increasing) order of importance. This could happen in an examination in First Aid, say, when it is obvious that, at the scene of a motor accident, it is more important to minimise a serious loss of blood than to put a splint on a broken finger!

Before leaving the 'list' type of question, a little more needs to be said about the remaining parts of such a question. Any simple list does not require much effort on the part of the candidate and the marks allocated will reflect this. Consequently, after a request for a list, a more searching question is often asked about one or more of the items in the list. Obviously, this is the major part of the question and it will carry the greater number of marks. So when reading a question relating to a list, make sure that you understand the rest of the question fully – and allocate enough time to it – for this is likely to be the most important part of it all.

▶ Survey ◀

The term 'survey' often has a similar meaning to 'list', but the context of the question will indicate the level of detail expected. Whereas a list can consist of single words or items, a survey is likely to involve rather more than that.

If, for example, a question asks you to 'survey as widely as possible' *and* if there are no other parts to the question, then the length of the list of items mentioned in the survey will dictate what is wanted of you.

Dealing with this type of topic in abstract terms is of little value, so let us look at a specific example. Home decoration.

Consider a question such as 'Survey, as widely as possible, the various factors involved in redecorating a room in the home'.

That question has vast scope. Matters such as the size of room; the cost of the paper, paint and other materials; the inconvenience to the occupants; the durability required (i.e. is it a bathroom needing wipe-down paper or a child's room which may require redecoration at

frequent intervals – for whatever reason). Does the
woodwork need repainting first? Does the ceiling also
need attention? All of these need to be mentioned, and
more, if the survey is to be sufficiently comprehensive to
gain a good examination score. With questions such as
this, you should be aware of the size that the survey can
reach.

This being the case, it is unlikely that great *detail* in
each of the items is called for and the time spent on each
item should be apportioned accordingly. Incidentally, for
your own sake, it could prove useful to draft a single-
word list of the items in addition to the survey in order to
keep a check on the size of the latter.

Alternatively, the question could be something more
like 'Survey the *aesthetic* factors which are involved in
the redecoration of a room in the home'.

The items in such a survey are, obviously, fewer in
number and hence much more detail will be required in
each aspect of the answer (that is, assuming that the
question has no other parts).

Answering this question will involve a rather more
detailed knowledge of the nature of decoration and the
functions it is intended to serve. Such factors as 'Does the
room have large or small windows?' and 'Do the windows face north or south?' play a part in the choice of
wallpaper or paint. If the windows are small and the room
faces north (in the northern hemisphere), then there
would be an advantage in having the paper pale in
colour, otherwise the room would run the risk of being
undesirably dark.

Other factors include the size of the room. If it is large,
then papers with a big, bold pattern with a long distance
between repeating themes can be used. In small rooms,
such papers could be disastrous (aesthetically). A lounge
in which people are going to sit for long periods will
appear to be physically cool if 'cold' colours such as blues
and greens are used, but in bathrooms, such colours may
be much more acceptable. And so on.

▶ Define ◀

In normal usage, the word 'define' has two meanings. It can relate to the specification of certain limits, e.g. 'Define the legal limits to which a person is permitted to go in order to expel an unwanted visitor from his home.' However, this is not the context most often met in examination papers.

For our purposes, 'define' is more often used in the context of a statement employed to describe a phenomenon or behaviour pattern, a substance, a law of nature or some other subject which, otherwise, would require a lengthy description. Definitions tend to be applied more to scientific and legal areas than to artistic ones.

Definitions are intended to be statements which specify certain facts with the greatest economy of words, but without sacrificing accuracy. For example, have you ever tried to describe (or 'define') a spiral, without using your hands? It is not easy and a dozen different people could, in writing, give a dozen different answers, none of them necessarily being perfect, or even accurate. (This particular definition becomes even more complex if the term 'helix' is used to define a spiral – the dictionary definition of 'helix' says that it is the same as a spiral!) Hence the need for a satisfactory, 'official' definition.

A question which asks 'Define . . .' usually requires the candidate to quote some standard statement. A simple quotation will earn a small number of marks on an exam paper (the number of marks being dependent on the complexity and accuracy of the definition). Many students simply memorise definitions without understanding their full implication. However, as the majority of marks are usually awarded for the answer to a separate part of the question, based on the *application* of the definition, an ignorance of the deeper significance of the definition can result in poor marks, even though the definition itself is recorded accurately.

An example familiar to most people is Archimedes'

Principle. It may be expressed in several ways, one of them being 'When an object is partly or totally immersed in a fluid, it is subjected to an upthrust equal to the weight of fluid displaced.'

The common mistake of substituting the word 'liquid', or even worse, 'water', for 'fluid' would gain little credit, as it would demonstrate to the examiner that the candidate did not fully understand the principle. The word 'fluid' applies to all substances which flow and that includes not only liquids but gases.

The terms 'partly' and 'totally' are equally important, especially where practical examples are concerned. Steel ships which float on water (their weight is referred to as 'displacement') and instruments such as hydrometers are examples of objects which, in normal use, are partly immersed in a fluid. Objects which are fully immersed in fluids include balloons filled with hydrogen, helium or hot air.

A thorough _understanding_ of the 'upthrust' concept can be used, by the candidate, to explain why some objects float and some sink, in gases as well as liquids. More importantly, it will give the candidate the means of answering questions on applications which he or she has never encountered previously. A candidate who had simply memorised the statement (or definition) parrot fashion would not be able to do this.

The same considerations apply to any topic encompassed by a 'definition', 'principle' or 'law'. Examine the statement, analyse exactly what each word or term means and then play the game of 'What if?' In other words, change the wording to see whether any significant change in meaning occurs. Try several different examples – extreme examples, and see what you learn. If you come across stumbling blocks which you can't overcome on your own, then ask someone.

Using the techniques described here should ensure that you can score high marks on any question relating to a 'law', 'principle' or 'definition'.

▶ Compare and Contrast ◀

Strictly speaking, the term 'compare' involves consideration of similarities *and* differences, whereas 'contrast' refers only to differences. However, the terms 'compare' and 'contrast' are often used together in examination questions and for convenience they will be grouped together here.

These terms are intended to test your depth of understanding of two or more items or topics of a similar nature.

A question such as 'Compare and contrast the use of public transport and your own private means of travel' could, depending upon the time available, be part of a question, or could be a full one in its own right.

As a full question, it would involve such similarities as what each does (gets you from A to B). Differences such as the initial outlay, running costs, convenience and ecological considerations would all need comment.

This would almost certainly mean the question was an essay type. If, on the other hand, a separate part of the question asked for more detailed information, you could probably answer the 'compare and contrast' section in tabular form: as a part question, it would correspond to a 'survey' to be answered in a simple fashion. The remainder of the question might well ask for a much more detailed account of some specific item (or items) mentioned in the first part.

▶ Discuss ◀

The term 'discuss' implies a detailed treatment of some specified topic. Sometimes, for added emphasis, you are asked to 'discuss in detail'. It is self-evident that such a question cannot be answered to the examiner's satisfaction by means of a table, as was the case in some of the previous examples. The very term 'discuss' implies the use of reasoned arguments. So we are looking at an essay-type answer.

If, on reading a question requiring 'discussion', you realise that you have given only superficial treatment to the subject in your revision, it would be prudent to avoid the question in favour of one for which you are better prepared. A 'discuss' type of question does require a good deal of understanding if a full and satisfactory answer is to be given.

A question such as 'Discuss the factors which govern the choice of a suitable household pet' can hardly be answered in a creditable manner by replying 'I *like* German Shepherd dogs'! Your answer would have to include such factors as where the pet is to live and hence how a dwelling in a high-rise block of flats would be unsuitable for large pets (such as German Shepherds). The answer should also include the type of pet which *would* be more suitable for such an environment, and consider other environments (e.g. houses with large gardens or country cottages) if it is to have sufficient scope to qualify as a good 'discussion', and hence gain good marks. In addition, a good answer to this question could not exclude other types of pets – cats, fish, birds and so on. Time would dictate whether more exotic pets should be included in the discussion (although a few seconds spent on a *brief* mention would not go amiss). Generally the examiner would be looking for a demonstration that you appreciate the *principles* involved.

▶ Describe and Explain ◀

These are two of the commonest terms used in examination papers, but they are often misunderstood or, at least, the cause of poor marks. It is quite amazing how many candidates confuse these two terms.

The word 'describe' means simply that. You should give a *description* of whatever is asked for. This requires no understanding, no logic and no deductions on your part. You can describe something simply from memory. Nothing more than that is needed.

'Explain' is totally different. To *explain* something

requires an understanding of the subject. Very often, of course, the term 'explain' will necessitate a description as well as the explanation.

'Explain' is really asking '*Why*' (e.g. is a piece of equipment built in that way, or used in that particular way)? In this context, 'Describe' is asking 'What' (does the equipment look like) or 'How' (do you use it).

The 'explain' type of question is intended to test your *understanding* of the subject rather than your memory and poorly prepared candidates will soon reveal their ignorance. By the same token, although such a question is more demanding, it does offer the well-prepared candidate the opportunity to excel. Even if you miss out the odd point, the examiner can read into your answer and see that the true understanding is there.

Let us take a look at an example of the differences between these two terms. A question on home decoration could be 'Describe the steps involved in papering a wall which has not been previously papered'. This question is simply asking for a description of the steps to be taken. These would include sizing the wall; marking a vertical line on the wall; cutting the paper into appropriate lengths; pasting the paper and applying the paper to the wall.

Note that the question, *as it stands*, is not particularly demanding. Had it been set as course work, the response could have been obtained from any standard text book, or DIY manual. No understanding of the *reasons* is asked for.

Now let us look at what would be required if the question used the word 'explain' instead of 'describe'.

Sizing the wall (i.e. applying a coating of adhesive well in advance of, and in addition to, the actual papering) would still need to be mentioned, but you would be expected to add the *reason* for this step, i.e. to prevent some of the water of the adhesive being absorbed into the untreated wall, which could possibly result in loss of adhesion. The *reasons* for marking a vertical line on the wall would need to be explained. Similarly, measuring the paper prior to cutting (taking into account the need for extra paper for the purposes of pattern matching when hanging the paper) would need to be covered. Details of allowing the paper to 'soak' and to expand, prior to hanging, would be expected. An explanation of *why* the paper needs to be applied from the top downwards; *why* the air bubbles need to be removed from between the paper and the wall – and hence *why* the paper needs to be brushed from the centre in an outward direction – and *why* patterns should be lined up would all need mention if good marks were to be won. Simply *describing* the actions involved would be inadequate in answer to a question which asks you to *explain*.

▶ Illustrate ◀

The principle behind the old saying 'a single picture is worth a thousand words' has never been more valuable than when it is applied in examination answers. Such requests as 'Illustrate your answer with a diagram' are commonplace in many examination questions. The use of diagrams, sketches and graphs can not only reduce the amount of writing that needs to be done, but it also indicates very clearly, and with economy of time and effort, your understanding of principles and/or concepts which would otherwise be extremely taxing to deal with under examination conditions.

A word of warning, though. When a topic is summarised by means of a diagram, it is a mistake to believe that the diagram is the be-all and end-all of the topic itself. Unless you fully understand the principles involved, it is easy to *assume* that a diagram will say everything you want it to say. The use of a diagram without adequate reference to it will not impress examiners. The illustration should be *in addition* to the answer, not a substitute for it.

A common error made with graphs is to omit labelling the axes. Without labelling *and* dimensions on the axes, graphs are useless. More importantly, an examiner will recognise an unlabelled graph not only as sloppy work

When a diagram alone is not the answer

Most people have heard of the Carbon Cycle – nature's way of 'recycling' the element carbon between plant and animal life. On one occasion when I was standing in for an absent colleague who taught Biology, I told the group of students that I was going to deal with the Carbon Cycle.

'Oh we've done that,' they retorted and, when I asked them what it was about, they replied, 'It's a diagram with lots of lines going in different directions.' When pressed, they mentioned that carbon dioxide was associated with some of those 'lines'.

To those students the diagram *was* the full subject. Had they used the diagram alone as an answer to a question asking for an illustrated *description* or *explanation* of the Carbon Cycle, they would have scored only the few marks allocated to the diagram.

They were taken aback when I posed the question, 'If countless millions of animals have been breathing in oxygen, and breathing out carbon dioxide, for countless millions of years, why hasn't the world's atmosphere run out of oxygen and why hasn't carbon dioxide accumulated in its place?'

They knew that *plants* performed the reverse process, i.e. took in carbon dioxide and 'breathed out' oxygen, but they hadn't really associated this phenomenon with nature's balance of oxygen and carbon dioxide over the ages. It was something of a revelation to them when I pointed out that the increasing world population *and* the increasing trend to burn carbon-based fuels *increases* the carbon dioxide content of the atmosphere and that destroying the tropical rain forests helps to *prevent the reverse process*. Most people nowadays are aware of the resulting increasing 'Greenhouse Effect'. The students knew each of the isolated facts, but they had not associated them as being a part of the Carbon Cycle.

> Whenever an examination question states 'Illus-
> trate your answer . . .', make sure that you pay due
> attention to the answer itself. The illustration should
> be just that – an illustration!

but also as the work of a candidate who may not understand the subject properly. Remember, it is up to *you* to
convince the examiner that you know what you are
writing about. He will not *assume* this automatically.

There is another interpretation of the word 'illustrate'
as used in examination questions. This applies when an
essay type of answer is called for and when diagrams or
graphs would not be appropriate. The *context* of the
question and the type of examination will dictate the
response required from the candidate. For example, a
question such as 'What safety measures should be taken
in the design and construction of buildings intended to be
used by the general public? Illustrate your answer with
specific examples' is not asking for diagrams of smoke
detectors or water sprinklers but rather *specific examples*
of, say, tragedies which could have been avoided had
such devices been installed (or, for example, if fire exits
had been better designed and signposted).

▶ Interpret ◀

In some respects, the term 'interpret' means the opposite
of 'illustrate'. In an examination question employing this
term, candidates will be given data, graphs or charts from
which they will be expected to make observations and
draw conclusions. Such questions can be quite searching
and, in some cases, *personal* interpretations may be
expected by the examiner. If you have not encountered
the proffered information before, the question can be
quite disconcerting. However, the well-prepared candidate should not allow himself to be adversely affected by
questions of this type.

Such questions are intended to test your *understanding*, rather than your memory, but this can be used to advantage. You could be 'wrong' in your interpretation of a set of facts, but unless you draw any conclusions that are *totally* illogical, you can score high marks. In fact, with questions such as these there is often no 'right' or 'wrong' answer! The following examples may serve to illustrate these points. Consider the following question:

'The table below shows the results of two consecutive elections. The figures are expressed as the percentage of votes gained by each of three candidates representing parties X, Y and Z. Interpret the figures from the standpoint of the candidate for party Z and comment on his possible future as a candidate for the constituency.'

	X	Y	Z
Previous election	50	40	10
Present election	45	35	20

Several interpretations of these results are possible. Let us look at a few of them.

1. Candidate Z may as well not bother to stand for election again. Even though he gained more votes in the recent election, he has the support of only one in every five of the electorate.
2. What a fantastic triumph for the candidate for party Z! He has doubled his popularity. If this trend continues then in the next election, party X will get 35 per cent, Y will get only 25 per cent and Z will romp home with 40 per cent of the votes.
3. If the increase in popularity of candidate Z continues at this pace, then he'll gain another 10 per cent of the votes in the next election. That means that he'll tie with candidate Y (with 30 per cent of the votes). X will still win, but it won't be the landslide that it was in the previous election.

Various other interpretations could involve the possibility of gaining extra votes exclusively from party X, or from party Y. Each interpretation is valid in its own way. None of them can be said to be 'wrong' and, therefore, each must gain some marks. It is unlikely that full marks would be gained by using any single interpretation. A variety of interpretations would be needed for that, but it does illustrate the point about 'right' and 'wrong' answers with this type of question.

The next example is quite different.

'In London in December 1952 (before the Clean Air Act was in force) the sulphur dioxide and smoke content of the atmosphere (caused by burning fossil fuels) peaked on the 7th and 8th days of the month and returned to their previous values by the 15th. During the same period of time, the deaths due to bronchitis, pneumonia and heart failure increased by a factor of more than three, peaking around the 9th of the month, but still being about twice the "normal" for that time of the year on the 15th. Interpret these facts in the context of the effect of sulphur dioxide and smoke on health.'

From the facts given, the effect of the atmospheric pollutants on human health is self-evident and it would be difficult to find more than one valid interpretation. For brevity, this question has been simplified somewhat. A full question would probably involve a graph, or the data needed to plot the graph, together with the requirement of a more detailed answer from the candidate.

▶ Other Terms ◀

In the preceding sections we have looked at some of the more common terms used in examination papers. The list is, obviously, not exhaustive, but the terms discussed above represent the essence of those that examiners use. Other terms are variations on the themes mentioned or, if not, their meanings should be obvious.

What is important is to assess what the examiner wants, and react accordingly. Hence, a question such as 'What events led to the start of World War I?' has to be taken in

the context of the rest of the exam paper. If this constitutes a full question, then the time you are expected to
spend on it is dictated by the time allowance for each
question (see Chapter 11). Alternatively, if it is only part
of a question, then the time to be spent will depend upon
the remaining parts of that same question (although in the
latter case, the brevity of the required reference to
'events' is likely to be qualified by such terms as 'survey',
'state' or 'summarise').

If the marks allocated to each part of a question are
indicated on the paper, the relative amounts of time to be
spent on each part will be dictated by the maximum
marks to be gained.

As stated in Chapter 10, you should be happy that you
understand the examiner's requirements clearly before
you attempt to answer a question.

Appendix 2

▼

Handling Formulae

Formulae are often given as a means of deriving 'answers' to a variety of problems. The advice offered is 'remember the formula'. My advice is, *don't* – unless there is absolutely no alternative. Instead, derive the formula from first principles. If you can't do it for yourself, then refer to text books and if they don't help, ask your teacher or tutor.

As an example, let us take the common formulae for converting the temperature scales of Fahrenheit and Celsius (or Centigrade). The 'simple' equations which we are often recommended to memorise are:

$$°F = (°C \times 9/5) + 32 \quad \text{and} \quad °C = (°F - 32) \times 5/9$$

Simple? Easy to remember during examination conditions? Hardly. Under examination conditions it is all too easy to ask yourself, 'Do I add 32 or subtract it? Do I do it at the start or at the end of the calculation? Do I multiply by 5/9 or 9/5?' The more you question yourself, the more you become sure that you have it wrong!

Temperature conversions are no different from many others. You need two pieces of information. The first is a *reference point* from which to measure (e.g. 'This point on the wall is 1.4 metres' – from where? The floor, the ceiling, the left-hand corner, the door jamb?). The second is a conversion factor (e.g. 1 gallon = 4.55 litres, or 1 inch = 25.4 millimetres).

First, let us consider the reference point. Imagine a thermometer shown diagrammatically, as in figure 1. Consider the reference point as being the temperature at which pure water freezes. The level of the mercury in the thermometer will be as shown in the diagram and this can be marked at the side of the thermometer itself. At the left-hand side the temperature will be marked as 0° on the Celsius scale. The *same* level marked on the right-hand side will correspond to 32° on the Fahrenheit scale. (I am assuming that you already know these temperatures, together with the boiling points of 100°C and 212°F respectively.)

It is important to note that from here on, *all* calculations will be taken from *these temperature reference points*.

Next, we need to obtain our conversion factors between the Celsius and Fahrenheit scales and to do this we need to consider a *rise* in temperature (from the freezing point).

Figure 1 (overleaf) shows that the *rise* in temperature from the freezing point to the boiling point of pure water is 100° on the Celsius or Centigrade scale ('centi' referring to 100 and 'grade' referring to the 'graduations'). On the Fahrenheit scale, the *same* temperature rise is 180° (212 minus 32).

Simplifying this by dividing both of these figures by 20 we arrive at the conclusion that a 5 degree rise on the Celsius scale corresponds to a 9 degree rise on the Fahrenheit scale. In other words:

A rise of 1 degree C = a rise of 9/5 degrees F and

a rise of 1 degree F = a rise of 5/9 degrees C

When the formula is derived in this way, it is *impossible* to get the fraction wrong!

Now let us get down to temperature conversions. Say 20° Celsius is to be converted to Fahrenheit. A temperature of 20°C corresponds to 20° *above the freezing point*. The calculation in figure 2 shows that this is the same as 36°F *above the freezing point*. However, as the freezing point on this scale is 32°, it follows that 20°C is the same temperature as 36°F *above the freezing point* of 32°F, i.e. is 68°F.

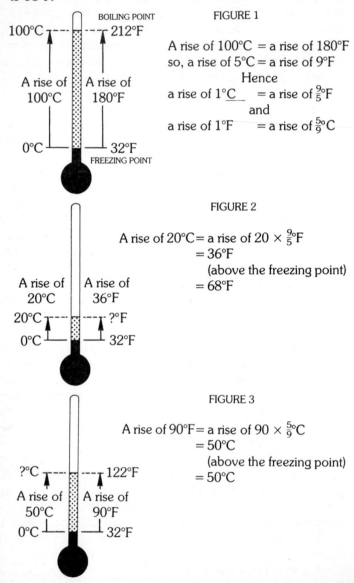

FIGURE 1

A rise of 100°C = a rise of 180°F
so, a rise of 5°C = a rise of 9°F
Hence
a rise of 1°C = a rise of $\frac{9}{5}$°F
and
a rise of 1°F = a rise of $\frac{5}{9}$°C

FIGURE 2

A rise of 20°C = a rise of 20 × $\frac{9}{5}$°F
= 36°F
(above the freezing point)
= 68°F

FIGURE 3

A rise of 90°F = a rise of 90 × $\frac{5}{9}$°C
= 50°C
(above the freezing point)
= 50°C

Once again, if this procedure is followed logically, then it is impossible for the calculation to be incorrect!

Conversion from the Fahrenheit to the Celsius scale is just as simple. As shown in figure 3, a temperature of 122°F is 90 degrees *above the freezing point* and 90 degrees on this scale is the same as 90 x 5/9 degrees on the Celsius scale, i.e. 50 degrees. In other words the temperature of 122°F is the same as 50°C.

▶ Other Formulae ◀

The example given above involves a fairly simple conversion from one temperature scale to another. Other conversions (e.g. imperial to metric) may involve units which can complicate matters somewhat, especially when the units are multiplied. Let me simplify this with an example. There is no problem when units of distance (or length) such as metres or miles are multiplied by a *number*. The product will still be expressed in metres or miles. However, when two measurements expressed in *units* are multiplied, then the product is in new units. Four metres multiplied by three metres produces twelve *square* metres and represents an *area* (e.g. of a floor). Similarly when three dimensions are multiplied, the result represents a *volume* and must be expressed in *cubic* form.

All this is self-evident but may not be quite so obvious when specific conversion formulae are employed. Let us take an example of formulae involving the conversion factor π as used in calculations involving circles. It gives the relationship between the radius of a circle and its circumference; the radius of a circle and its area, and the radius of a sphere and its volume.

The following formulae are well known, but remember that it is the *principle* which is important here. It is possible to identify what a formula represents simply by studying it. It should not be necessary for you to have to *remember* whether it deals with a distance, an area or a volume. Take the following as examples:

a. $\pi \times D$ (or $2\pi \times r$)   b. $\pi \times r^2$ c. $\frac{4}{3}\pi r^3$

In these formulae, π is a _number_ and therefore does not affect the units used in the calculation (as mentioned above) nor does any other number used in the formulae. Hence, if 'r' is expressed in linear dimensions such as metres, then the effect of multiplying 'r' by a _number_ (including π) will be to give a linear product, i.e. a number of metres.

Now let us look at each of the formulae above:

a. This consists of one dimension ('r' or 'D' expressed in linear units such as metres) multiplied by the number π. The result of the calculation must, therefore, be in the form of the original dimension, i.e. in metres. It is the _circumference_ of a circle.

b. This consists of a dimension ('r') multiplied by another dimension ('r'), hence the product of the calculation must be expressed as an _area_, e.g. as square metres (expressed as m^2). The formula is that for calculating the _area_ of a circle.

c. As this formula involves the product of three dimensions ('r' in each case) then the product of any calculation based on this formula must give rise to a _volume_ (e.g. cubic metres – expressed as m^3).

▶ Converting Units ◀

The principles mentioned above give a basis for converting any measurement from one kind of unit into another (e.g. imperial into metric). One example should suffice to demonstrate this point. Let us take the linear units of miles and kilometres. As a practical working approximation, 5 miles is equivalent to 8 kilometres, so we can deduce that 1 mile = $\frac{8}{5}$ kilometres, i.e. 1.6 kilometres. Similarly, 1 kilometre = $\frac{5}{8}$ miles, i.e. 0.625 miles. One square mile is, therefore, 1.6 x 1.6 square kilometres, i.e. 2.56 km^2 and one square kilometre is the same area as 0.625 x 0.625 square miles, i.e. 0.39 square miles.

Conversion of virtually any other set of units can be achieved by using similar methods.

Appendix 3

▼

The Driving Test

Although the driving test is predominantly practical in nature, it is, nevertheless, an examination and can be tackled with the help of the techniques described in this book. Such matters as satisfactory preparation, understanding and 'nerves' apply equally to the driving test as to more academic pursuits. One thing is different though. After passing an examination you may, if you wish, forget the subject material which you learned. With driving, your ability to ensure your own safety, and that of others, will be under test every time you drive a vehicle.

No book can teach you how to drive any more than it can teach you how to swim, ride a bicycle or play the piano. To develop practical skills such as these, you will need to practise. But the driving test is devised to assess whether you are a sufficiently good driver to be allowed to drive on the public highways without supervision. In other words, it is intended to test your driving *technique*. Many people can learn to handle the *mechanical* aspects of driving a car (or motorcycle) but this does not mean that they will become competent drivers. To repeat the comments made in the Introduction, it is not what you do, it is the way that you do it!

The importance of a good driving technique cannot be overemphasised. In a supermarket you may, absent-mindedly, block other shoppers' paths or even run your trolley into theirs. A simple 'Sorry!' is all that is needed to excuse a momentary lack of concentration. A lack of concentration when you are in control of a vehicle could mean that your 'Sorry' is uttered in a hospital or a police station. Or both.

▶ Good Driving ◀

The process of learning to drive *well* is a continuous one. It can last a lifetime. Some people never manage it. Your aim, as a learner driver, should not be simply to pass the test, although this is probably the immediate target. The aim should be to become a good driver, and by adopting correct attitudes *at the outset*, your likelihood of success in the test itself will be increased.

The question 'What is a good driver?' is not an easy one to answer in simple terms. One adequate definition is 'a driver who does not force another driver to change direction, speed or gear'. It is not a perfect definition, but it does illustrate an important point: that a good driver is not an isolated person, but one of many who, simultaneously, share the roads. In *safety*.

The purpose of this section is not to repeat the information given in the *Highway Code*, which is often confusing to the learner. It is to explain *why* some of the rules you have to learn have been formulated. Once you understand why, the rest will seem like common sense, as indeed it should be.

▶ The Learner's Advantage ◀

Odd as it may seem, the learner has a considerable advantage over the more practised driver. How often have you witnessed a driver doing something stupid and thought, 'I don't know how he passed his test'? Occasionally, the driver may have *only just* passed the test but, more often (if my observations are anything to go by), the driver is a mature one and, presumably, has had more experience. Many drivers regard themselves as being beyond criticism once they have passed their test. They ignore bad habits because they don't realise that they are practising them. The habits become worse and bad drivers collect more of them because they *don't care*!

The learner driver needs, by law, to have a qualified supervisor, tutor or teacher. It is worthwhile getting a good one because any habits picked up at the beginning are likely to be retained for a lifetime – especially bad ones! While under instruction for driving it is important that you do not resent any criticism. Instead, accept it and analyse it *in detail*. If you have made some blunder, find out not only *what* it is, but, more importantly, *why*, because every time you correct some imperfection in technique, you become a better driver.

▶ Mechanical and Mental Matters ◀

During the first few attempts at driving, the beginner often doubts whether he will ever master the process. There seem to be so many actions that need to be performed. There can't be many learners who haven't tried to move off without engaging first gear – well, at least once.

After plenty of practice, these matters resolve themselves and the more advanced learner manages to regard the mechanics of driving almost as second nature. This is the time when the *mental* processes should start to be trained, for it is the mental attitude to driving which distinguishes the good drivers from the bad.

▶ Don't assume! ◀

If there were a handful of 'rules' that could be used to improve a learner's technique, one of the more important ones would be 'Don't assume'. Don't *assume* that there is no traffic approaching at the next junction; don't *assume* that the nearest pedestrian isn't going to step off the pavement; don't *assume* that the driver of the car which has just stopped ahead of you isn't going to open his door as you are passing and, above all, don't *assume* that it is safe to overtake! With potential hazards such as these, and many, many more, always *make sure* first.

Actually, there is one exception to this rule: you can *always* assume that other road users (including pedestrians) are going to do something silly. I know that this sounds cynical but if you are prepared for such events, and drive in a defensive manner, you will be able to avoid the potential dangers to which less careful drivers fall victim.

A further word of warning. A safe and careful driver is *not* one who always drives excessively slowly in order to avoid dangers. That technique annoys other drivers and prompts them to take risks to overtake in order to avoid being held up unreasonably. However, a safe but adequate speed is something that can be judged only with experience. This will come in time and with practice.

▶ The 'Rules of the Road' ◀

At first sight, the 'rules' in the *Highway Code* appear formidable. How can you remember about 200 dos or don'ts and possibly answer questions about them during the driving test? My response to that is, *Don't* try to memorise those rules! In the same way that I have advised you not to try to remember hundreds of facts for written examinations, I repeat, 'Don't remember. Instead, *understand*!'

Imagine that you are taking your driving test and the examiner asks you, 'Where must you not overtake?' What he is *not* asking for is an answer like this: 'On a pedestrian crossing; near a hump-backed bridge; when approaching a school-crossing patrol; wait a minute, there's some more – oh yes, at a level crossing – I know there are more, I'll think of them in a minute. . . .' Such a response illustrates that the driver being tested does not *understand* what is wanted and is not likely to impress the examiner favourably.

To deal in detail with every one of the 'rules' in the *Highway Code* would take a full book the size of this one.

Instead, let me select a single example relating to over-taking and attempt to illustrate what is expected of a learner driver who hopes to pass the test. But first, what is wrong with the response quoted above? It is possible that, eventually, you *may* quote all the examples of situations when you should not overtake, but how long will it have taken? If you had been travelling along a fast stretch of road at, say, 60 mph and considering that it may have taken you about fifteen seconds to recite (and I repeat, *recite*) the rules, you would have covered a *quarter of a mile* before your answer was completed. Imagine travelling that distance, and at 60 mph, before you made a decision! The point is, you need to make decisions virtually *instantaneously* if you are to drive satisfactorily (especially at speed). So, what is the alternative to remembering that long list of 'rules'? Here is the answer. When considering those 'rules', don't try to memorise them. Instead, ask yourself a single question, 'Why is there a need for this?', or, simply, 'What if?'

▶ What if? ◀

Let us continue with the example about overtaking, although the *same technique* will apply to any other situation that is likely to crop up during the driving test. Use it. The principle is that the 'rules' are really common sense. They have been written over a long period of time as a result of some driver making a mistake and being involved in an accident, after which the 'rule' becomes obvious: 'If he had not done (whatever it was), then the accident would not have happened.'

Here is our example. You are travelling along a road and there is a vehicle ahead of you, travelling at about 30 mph. The road ahead seems to be clear of oncoming traffic and the road is wide enough for you to overtake. Now, is it safe for you to do so? Before you read on, think about it *carefully*, then answer.

The question seems to be a very easy one, but it is

more complicated than it may appear initially. If you answered with a simple 'Yes', then, I'm afraid, no marks!

Let us analyse the situation because, *as it is stated*, you don't have enough information to make a sound judgement about the question asked. You have probably 'assumed'!

Firstly, I haven't mentioned whether the road is subject to a speed limit. If a limit of 30 mph applies, the answer is utterly clear. You must *not* overtake! You would be breaking the law if you did so. Award yourself full marks if you spotted this one – but don't get too confident just yet.

Another question. Does the presence of 30 mph signs mean that it is safe for you to drive at 30 miles per hour? The answer is 'Not necessarily'. The 30 mph sign indicates the *maximum* speed at which you are permitted to drive. The road conditions and circumstances dictate the *actual* speed at which it is safe to drive. Such matters as the proximity of a pedestrian crossing, traffic congestion and the presence of children on the pavements all contribute to the considerations of whether 30 mph is a safe speed (for others as well as yourself). If in doubt, ask yourself whether it is safe to encounter a roundabout at that speed. And all this applies to *perfect* driving conditions. In wet, slippery or icy conditions, speed of 30 mph could be utterly reckless.

Before we go any further, there is a warning to be given. If, at this moment, you are only beginning to learn to drive, and the mechanical aspects of driving are still giving you some problems, I would suggest that you leave the following questions until later, when you are happier with that part of driving. If, on the other hand, you are feeling more confident about handling a car, then, by all means, proceed.

I want you to use your imagination. You may have regarded the question as a simple exercise about remembering the *Highway Code*. Now what I want you to do is imagine that it is not a theoretical question, but instead, that you are at the wheel of a car, in a real-life situation. *Imagine* the road, and the vehicle ahead. Create, as far as

The Two-Second Rule

Learner drivers often lack the experience needed to judge stopping distances satisfactorily, so here the 'two-second rule' can be brought into play.

When the vehicle ahead passes some stationary object such as a telegraph pole or lamp post, start counting, at a normal talking speed, saying 'one thousand and one, two thousand and two . . . . The time between the first 'one' and the second 'two' is approximately two seconds and if you pass the same stationary object before your second 'and', then you are too close. Pull back!

All this applies under *perfect conditions*. Your vehicle must be in good condition, especially the brakes and tyres, *and* you should be fully alert and concentrating on the job of driving. Anything which impairs judgement or reaction times (such as tiredness, drugs or alcohol) will also affect stopping distances adversely. A vehicle with a heavy load and/or filled with passengers will require a greater distance in which to stop safely, as will any vehicle on road surfaces which are wet, icy or otherwise less than ideal.

you can, a full image of everything around you. OK? Now let's continue.

We will change the conditions a little. The difference this time is that the road has a 40 mph speed limit. *Now* is it safe to overtake?

I don't blame you if you hesitate to answer this one. Actually, you *still* don't have enough information. For example, how far behind the vehicle are you? A general recommendation is that, when following another vehicle, you should use the 'two-second rule' (explained in the

box above). There are at least two reasons for this One
is braking distance. If, for any reason, the vehicle ahead
brakes suddenly, you will need this distance to stop in
safety. Incidentally, this spacing between your vehicle
and the one ahead is the minimum *under good conditions* and this expression refers both to your vehicle
(including tyres) and to the road. In wet conditions it is
advisable to double this distance, and increase it even
further on icy roads.

The second reason concerns vision. The closer you are
to the vehicle in front, the less you will be able to see
ahead, and this includes such things as approaching
traffic and road signs. This is particularly important if the
vehicle ahead is a large one such as a van or coach.

In order to overtake the vehicle in front safely, you
need to be able to see whether the road ahead is clear. If
you are *already* travelling at 40 mph (i.e. if you don't have
to accelerate to this speed from 30 mph), it will take
approximately eight seconds to draw level with the vehicle
from a distance of about 36 metres behind. It will need a
further eight seconds to move far enough ahead of it to
pull in to your original distance from the nearside kerb in
safety. The total distance involved for this full manoeuvre
is almost 290 metres (or about 950 feet). Therefore, you
will need to be able to see *at least* this distance ahead in
order to avoid a *stationary* object! A vehicle travelling
towards you can double or treble this distance – or even
more depending upon its speed. Hence, the question is,
can you see that far ahead? Does the road bend to
obscure your vision? Is it foggy? Such questions, and
more, *must* be brought into the equation so, if there is
any doubt, *any doubt at all*, don't overtake.

Before we get to the topic of road signs mentioned
earlier, let us consider another aspect of the same situation. This time let us imagine that you are on a dual
carriageway. You may think that the problem with
oncoming traffic is eliminated. There can't be any
oncoming traffic because it would be on the other side of
the central division. Does this mean that it is now totally

Beware Statistics!

Many people are eager to give advice on driving. Some advice is sound, some less so. To be sure of the validity of such advice, always ask 'Why?' because the *reasons* for a statement are often more important than the statement itself. Advice which is particularly prone to being misunderstood is that which is based on statistics. For example, you may be told that '99 times out of 100 it is safe' to do something or other. Such a statement *may* be true, but that does not mean that you get 99 'free goes'. The single occasion (out of 100) when an accident is likely to occur *could be* occasion number 100, but, equally, it could be occasion number 50. By the same rule it could be occasion number 1. So you have been warned!

---

safe for you to overtake? OK, you've guessed it. Of course it doesn't!

▶ Is it ever safe to overtake? ◀

From the comments above, it might appear that it is *never* safe to overtake but this is, of course, not true. The object of these little mental exercises is to make you appreciate the potential problems with the process of overtaking. An advantage of this question-and-answer approach is that, once you have worked out the answers, you won't have to remember them! They will have become a part of your inherent understanding of the hazards of driving. They will become second nature (or, if you prefer it, common sense) to you. So far, we have touched upon twenty items in the *Highway Code* but, because we have been treating them as potential practical problems, rather than 'dos' and 'don'ts', you may not have noticed this. If you treat all of the other 'rules' in the same way, then you won't need to try to memorise them.

Now let us get back to our dual carriageway. If you have been following the vehicle closely, then, as stated before, your view of the road conditions ahead will be restricted and you will be unable to gather enough information to consider the existing hazards adequately. If you drive a good distance behind the vehicle, your view will be better and so will your information intake.

At this point, I want you to stretch your imagination a little further. You are still driving along that dual carriageway, ready to overtake the vehicle in front, but this time I want you to imagine that you are *also* in a helicopter looking down on your own progress. In this way, you can consider those hazards from a more advantageous viewpoint.

Right, then, you can look down and see yourself behind the vehicle. You have pulled out slightly, so as to see the road ahead. As it is a dual carriageway, there is no oncoming traffic so it seems safe for you to overtake. You start to do so. From your position on the road, the vehicle ahead obscures some of your view of the near-side part of the road and the nearer you are to the vehicle ahead, the more your view is obscured. For example, from the driving position, you can't see the cyclist ahead, so you proceed to overtake. Now, from your elevated position in the helicopter, you can see that the driver of the vehicle in front is going to pull away from the near side so as to avoid the cyclist (or any type of obstruction). Your reaction from your aerial position is to scream, 'Don't overtake!' Your reaction from the *driving* position might be to direct some uncomplimentary remarks at the driver of the vehicle ahead! After all, it was stupid of him to pull out when you were overtaking him.

Wait a minute, though. You expected *him* to use his mirrors to check that you were overtaking him. But did *you* use your mirrors for the same purpose? Some other driver might have been preparing to overtake you. The

Keep your eyes open

Did you know that the most common reason for learner drivers failing their test is lack of *effective observation* at junctions?

problem with vision, mentioned earlier, does not refer simply to vision ahead. To be a good driver, you need to be aware of *everything* around you. Not only ahead, but behind as well. That is why mirrors are compulsory in vehicles. And that is why you will be tested on your *use of mirrors* during your driving test. Think about it. It *is* important. Better still, *do it*. Use the mirrors all the time when you are driving.

I mentioned road signs earlier. The importance of some of them is obvious, but others? For example, those signs which show that there is a minor road joining the near side of the major road which you are on. So what?

Let us drive on an open road. Not much traffic about. All is well and there's not much that can go wrong. You can see that the road ahead is totally clear, and there is no vehicle behind, so it seems to be quite safe for you to overtake the vehicle ahead. From your position behind the wheel it doesn't seem to matter about signs relating to minor roads. If the vehicle ahead is a large one, you may not even have *noticed* the sign, on the near side, as you accelerate to overtake.

Suppose there is another vehicle on that side road, approaching the road which you are on. Also, suppose that the driver is one of those who drive as fast as possible and leave the process of braking until the very last moment. The driver of the vehicle in front of you may well think that the driver of the side road is not going to stop in time, or, perhaps, is going to try to rush out in front of him. He may brake suddenly, or he may even change lanes in order to avoid a collision. And during this time you will be overtaking! The *Highway Code* is quite clear about such a situation. *Don't overtake when approaching a junction*.

Now let us change the circumstances a little. This time, suppose that the driver ahead of you has signalled that he is going to turn into a nearside minor road. The driver in the side road will see this. Just as you may not be able to see him, equally he will not be able to see you either! If he intends to join the road that you are on and travel in the opposite direction to yours, he may not stop at the major road, but simply drive straight on to it. And you could be in the process of overtaking!

Whether it was another driver or whether it was you on that side road, the message should be absolutely clear. When approaching a major road, *stop* (there will be a sign to tell you so). Don't assume and don't proceed until you *know* that it is safe to do so.

▶ Signals ◀

The need for the constant use of mirrors has already been dealt with. Signals are equally important. When any change in direction is intended, signal to that effect. Before you intend to overtake, first use the mirror to confirm that it is safe, and then signal. Do the same when you have completed the manoeuvre, but *don't forget to cancel that signal*, otherwise, at the next nearside junction, a driver waiting to join your road may think that you are going to turn into his side road. You cannot blame him, because you will be signalling to that effect!

▶ Final Comments ◀

While the section has covered only a small fraction of the potential hazards associated with driving, I hope that it has indicated the *reasons* for the 'Rules of the Road'. Let me stress that you should not simply try to remember each 'rule' but rather, imagine yourself in the situation. Imagine that other road users are going to do something silly (as many will do!) and then consider the steps you should take to avoid becoming a victim of such ill-considered behaviour. In each of the examples above, don't leave the situation as it was described, but put yourself in the *other driver's* position. Imagine yourself to be the driver who you intend to overtake, and the driver on the side road. Always ask yourself 'What if?' and consider, in turn, the permutations of the results of each driver's possible actions.

Whenever you see a dangerous situation develop on the road, ask yourself how it originated, and, more importantly, what steps should have been taken to avoid it.

The constant use of these mental exercises will develop your understanding of the 'Rules of the Road'. They will cease to be an apparently endless list of 'dos' and 'don'ts' which need to be memorised. Instead they will become so self-evident that you will wonder how it was that you didn't think of them all by yourself! Understand those rules and practise them, for if you do, you will progress-ively become a better driver. And if you are a good driver, then you won't fail your driving test!

Appendix 4

▼

Relaxation Techniques

Many people find it difficult to relax under normal circumstances, but with examinations impending, the situation becomes more extreme. Comments such as 'Don't worry' or 'Don't take it so seriously' do little to help and, for many, the only way to avoid excessive anxiety is by making a concerted effort. But how?

There are many methods which can be used to assist relaxation. Some are quite casual. Others can virtually form the basis of a religion and demand a lifetime of dedication. The exercises which follow can be used or discarded at will, but I have found them to be of personal value for over forty years. I am still using some of them, as are others with whom I have shared my experiences. Some parts of the exercises may overlap with long-established practices. Other aspects may be new. What I do know is that they *work*!

▶ Outside the Examination Room ◀

When you are waiting to go into an examination room there is little on which the mind can focus and it is tempting to examine yourself on all aspects of the course material. The advice given in Chapter 6 is worth repeating here. It is, *Don't!* Don't discuss potential questions with fellow candidates; don't discuss statistics about which topics may crop up on the paper; don't discuss what you know or don't know and, above all don't ask yourself, 'What do I know about . . . ?'

So much for the negatives. Throughout this book, emphasis has been placed on being *positive* in your preparation. Be positive immediately before examinations also. It may be tempting to say 'I'm not going to fail this exam', but even this statement involves the possibility of failure. It includes negatives such as 'not' and 'fail'. The technique to employ is to tell yourself 'I am going to *pass* this exam.' Keep relaxed and stress this to yourself. Repeat it as often as necessary. You have every reason to believe it. Remember, you have done as much as possible to prepare for this exam and there is *no reason whatsoever* why you should not come through with flying colours.

▶ Waiting for the Paper ◀

Another time when anxiety can grow is when you are seated in the examination room, waiting to see the paper. There is no reason for concern. You are well prepared. *Take deep breaths.* This is important. Then clear your mind of any thoughts that could possibly be negative. Rest assured, once you get sight of the paper, you will be so busy reading and answering it that you will not have *time* for 'nerves' to take hold. Remember, the problem of 'nerves' is all in the mind, and you are the one in charge of that. Therefore, you are the one with all the advantages. Use them to your own benefit.

▶ Physical Relaxation ◀

The occasions described above occupy only a very small fraction of the academic year, but the anxiety brought about by examinations can start long before the examinations themselves. Pre-examination 'nerves' can attack, to a greater or lesser extent, weeks or even months prior to the examinations, so steps to counter such problems should be taken as early as possible. However, mental relaxation is very difficult, if not impossible, to achieve if the body is not also relaxed, so the process of relaxing the body should be made the first priority.

The following exercise is best practised while lying in bed, but this is not absolutely essential. In my early part-time student days, out of necessity, I have performed it lying on a workbench and, on occasions, even on the floor. For obvious reasons, a bed is better.

Lie on your back with your arms at your sides. Don't clench your fists but rather leave your hands open with palms facing downwards. Close your eyes and make sure that you are *totally* comfortable before proceeding any further. If *anything* feels uncomfortable, then take measures to rectify the situation.

Now, concentrate on your feet. Their position is not important as long as you feel comfortable. Let your feet sink into the bed. Relax your toes and let all feelings flow away. It should be possible to concentrate on relaxing your toes to such an extent that you cannot feel them. Proceed to your feet. They should follow until you are aware of no feeling there either. You should not even be aware of the pressure of your feet on the bed. They should, to all intents and purposes, not be there.

Don't worry about this experience. You will be in *total* control and at any time you wish, you will be able to bring the feeling back in a fraction of a second. You will always be in control, but a loss of feeling, under these circumstances, is always a disturbing experience initially. In time, you will accept this state of affairs as quite normal, but for the moment, if you have the slightest doubt, check that you can bring them back to 'life' in an instant. Then carry on, as before.

To proceed, once all feeling in your feet has disappeared, simply allow the lack of feeling to progress, slowly, further up your legs.

When you attempt this for the first time, it may require several minutes to allow the lack of feeling to reach your knees but, with practice, you will be able to master it in a matter of seconds. However, it does demonstrate how tense you are under 'normal' circumstances.

Let me interrupt myself here. The process of total relaxation is so alien to many people that, with beginners, by the time a loss of feeling has reached the lower body, the feet will have tied themselves in knots with muscular tension! If this is the case, there is only one way to progress. Go back to the beginning and start again. Believe me, it will be worth it.

After a number of attempts, it should be possible to clear all feeling from the whole body so that you will be lying almost in a state of suspended animation. The difference is that you will still be in total control of yourself and can revert back to 'normality' whenever you wish.

With plenty of practice, the technique of reaching *total body* relaxation should take no more than a minute or two from the beginning of the exercise, but the amount of practice it takes to achieve this depends upon the individual. Some people are normally tense, others can relax more easily. It all depends on you. One thing I will say, and here I make no apologies for repeating myself: for *your* sake, persevere with this exercise. It will give you more benefit than you can possibly imagine, and that is a promise!

▶ Mental Relaxation ◀

In some respects, mental relaxation is even more difficult than physical relaxation. Most people enjoy thinking about things. Often enough, they enjoy thinking about problems.

But we have the ability to be extremely selective in the things we think about. One example should be enough to demonstrate this. Whenever you are in a crowded place, a party, a disco or something like that, have you noticed your ability to home in on a particular conversation? It doesn't matter how much distraction there is in the form of other conversations or music, you can cut those out and concentrate on something which is of specific interest. Correct? Under such circumstances you are able to eliminate *anything* which is of no immediate interest.

With mental relaxation, you eliminate *everything* as being of no immediate interest.

As stated earlier, there is little point in trying to relax the mind if the body is not also relaxed, so start with that first. You will probably already have discovered that, once the body is fully relaxed, the brain tends to go into hyperdrive. All sorts of things seem to demand attention and it is this trend which is in need of control. It is quite pointless to tell yourself to stop thinking about whatever is occupying your thoughts because as soon as you eliminate one topic, another one will leap in to take its place. This is, of course, quite natural. During all your conscious moments, your brain is processing masses of information sent in via all of the five senses. This is a part of the brain's natural function and the object of this exercise is to give the brain a rest from this process. (Incidentally, the brain also works in a similar fashion when you are unconscious, i.e. asleep, but there is little that you can do to change that, even if you wanted to.)

Back to the process of relaxing the mind. You are lying with your body totally relaxed, but your brain is absorbed in thinking of all sorts of things. Even though your eyes are closed, you will probably be able to see images of some sort or another and it is this imagery that you need to eliminate.

Imagine that in the centre of your field of vision there is a tiny spot which is absolutely black. Not dark grey. Absolutely black. The image which you need to develop is exactly the opposite of what you would see if you were at the front of a train travelling through a tunnel. In this case, everything would be black, but at the end of the tunnel, far ahead, would be a spot of light. The spot of light will grow in size and your concentration will be focused on that ever-increasing area of interest.

At this moment, your total area of 'vision' is full of

interest and you need to remove that interest. It is practically impossible to do this all at once, so you will have
to do it gradually, hence the black spot. Allow the spot of
total blackness to grow in size slowly. As this happens, the
lighter areas containing images of interest will be reduced
in size and gradually pushed towards the edges of your
mental view. Remember, the spot is *totally* black. There
is no mark on it. No variation in colour or texture. It is
totally black and cannot be associated with any mental
picture.

The object of this exercise is to fill your field of vision
with blackness and, with it, total loss of thoughts. It may
take some minutes to achieve this, and it is unlikely that
you will be able to do it at the first attempt. Like all things
that are worthwhile, it requires effort. You are certain to
find that, after a bit of progress in clearing your mind of
thoughts, some little topic will crop up, demanding attention. *Eliminate it!* Don't let *any* thought get in the way.
The object is to clear your mind totally. Not even the
slightest idea should be admitted. No thoughts of any
kind.

Once you have mastered the technique of relaxing
both the body and the mind, you are likely to find that
you can time your period of relaxation. I used to practise
this during my lunch hour and found that I could judge
thirty minutes fairly accurately. After about half a minute,
I would be totally relaxed. During this time I would be
aware of what was going on around me, but would not
allow myself to think about it. After the predetermined
thirty minutes, some sort of inexplicable, built-in alarm
clock would warn me of the time, and I would return to
full consciousness. You should be able to do the same –
with a certain amount of practice, that is.

A word of warning. Once you end your state of relaxation, don't leap up into full activity. Allow your body and
mind a few minutes to come back to its normal state.
'Come around' slowly, for there is no point in subjecting
your entire system to an instantaneous switch from one
extreme to the other.

▶ Countering Insomnia ◀

A common problem with students is the inability to sleep when examinations are imminent. There seems to be so many things to worry about: so many problems, so many questions to be asked and answered. It is not surprising that sleep is elusive.

Providing that you have mastered the relaxation techniques described above, the answer to insomnia is fairly simple. Moreover, the technique can be used at any time in life and under virtually any circumstances. Troubles come all through life and this is one way in which you can prevent them from robbing you of your sleep.

If you suffer from insomnia, for whatever reason (except, of course, when you have already enjoyed a sufficiency of sleep) then three simple steps should rectify the situation. Firstly, relax the physical body as described above. Then relax the mind. Finally, after four or five minutes of total relaxation, on your back, change to your favourite sleeping position. Ensure that you are totally comfortable. Take care to avoid any position which allows you to hear, or feel, your pulse or heart beat. Then breathe in deeply, saying to yourself, 'Sleep.' Repeat this as you breathe out. Continue this process as you inhale and exhale. Don't allow *any* thought to enter your head.

If you follow this process faithfully, then you should find that the next experience is one of waking up, fully rested!

▼

Index